ADVANCE PRAISE FOI

*Meeting God in the Upper* . .......

"Like many of you, I always await Msgr. Vaghi's next book.... Sure enough, this one's another winner, as he takes us to where it all began, the Upper Room, the scene of the Last Supper and Pentecost. This work inspires the kind of meditation encouraged by St. Ignatius and his son, Pope Francis, as we prayerfully imagine ourselves in a biblical scene."

—Cardinal Timothy Michael Dolan, archbishop of New York

"Msgr. Peter Vaghi's journey into 'the most important room in Christendom' is a journey into the heart of the Church and the heart of Jesus. Along the way, Monsignor Vaghi offers practical wisdom for modern disciples. *Meeting God in the Upper Room* is contemporary spiritual writing at its finest."

—Matt Malone, SJ, editor-in-chief of *America* magazine

"As each follower of Jesus recognizes the call to be an evangelizing disciple, we take on the responsibility of renewing our faith, of standing firm in the conviction of its truth and finally of sharing it. Msgr. Vaghi provides guidance and support for all three of those elements in the life of the Christian today who truly wants to take on the mission that came to life in the Upper Room. We should all be grateful to Monsignor Vaghi for offering us this opportunity to spiritually visit the Upper Room and draw strength and inspiration from our encounter with God in that sacred space."

—Cardinal Donald Wuerl, archbishop of Washington, from the foreword

"*Meeting God in the Upper Room* is a book to grow in faith and the love of Jesus Christ. In a narrative both human and spiritual, well grounded in Scripture and key documents of the Church, Msgr. Peter Vaghi takes the reader into the heart of the Upper Room in Jerusalem, which witnessed central acts of Jesus.... Dare to be transformed by these pages."

—Mary Shivanandan, STD, author and former professor of theology, John Paul II Institute for Studies on Marriage & Family at the Catholic University of America

"In *Meeting God in the Upper Room,* Msgr. Vaghi weaves together Church Teachings, the creed, Church history, the Gospels, the necessity for service and evangelization, and he does this seamlessly with the constant backdrop of that Upper Room where the ministry and mission of the Church began. This book will take you there, to that room, and you will exit that place ready to walk in the footsteps of Jesus and the apostles. You will want to buy this book for a friend, but you will definitely want to keep your own copy so that you can reread it any time you seek another Upper Room moment."

—Denise Bossert, author, *Gifts of the Visitation*,
former public relations director of Israel Ministry of Tourism,
and founder of the apostolate *Holy Land on My Own*

"Msgr. Vaghi's new focus on the Upper Room and the salvation events that happened there gives a freshness to the familiar texts of the Last Supper and the resurrection. By drawing us back to the room where Christ gave us salvation, we are present again at his invitation to a follow him and to see anew the unfolding of his extraordinary gift. An evangelizing treasure!"

—Mary Ellen Bork, writer and lecturer on Catholic culture at
*Women for Faith & Family*

"I have read with admiration this new book, in which…the Upper Room becomes the amazing single locus for the central mysteries of our faith—then and now. The invitation to the reader to enter his or her own 'upper room' makes it a contemporary reality for every Christian. I especially enjoyed the frequent references to Pope Francis—they give the presentation a unifying voice. I am certain the book will have wide relevance for the new evangelization that is still unfolding in the Church."

—Monsignor Charles M. Murphy, author and former rector
of Pontifical North American College in Rome

MEETING GOD IN THE UPPER ROOM

# MEETING GOD IN THE UPPER ROOM

## Three Moments to Change Your Life

MONSIGNOR PETER J. VAGHI

servant
AN IMPRINT OF
FRANCISCAN MEDIA
Cincinnati, Ohio

Cover design by Candle Light Studio
Book design by Mark Sullivan

LIBRARY OF CONGRESS CATALOGING-IN-PUBLICATION DATA
Names: Vaghi, Peter J., author.
Title: Meeting God in the Upper Room : three moments to change your life / Peter J. Vaghi.
Description: Cincinnati : Servant, 2017. | Includes bibliographical references and index.
Identifiers: LCCN 2016043177 | ISBN 9781632531261 (trade paper : alk. paper)
Subjects: LCSH: Jesus Christ. | Catholic Church—Doctrines. | Catholic Church—Customs and practices. | Cenacle (Jerusalem)
Classification: LCC BT205 .V25 2017 | DDC 232.9/57—dc23
LC record available at https://lccn.loc.gov/2016043177

Published by Servant
an imprint of Franciscan Media
28 W. Liberty St.
Cincinnati, OH 45202
www.FranciscanMedia.org

Printed in the United States of America.
Printed on acid-free paper.

17 18 19 20 21  5 4 3 2 1

*I dedicate this book to my parishioners at the Church of the Little Flower in Bethesda, Maryland, where I have been pastor for twelve years.*

*In addition, I dedicate this book to the members of the John Carroll Society in this my thirtieth year of service as chaplain.*

# CONTENTS

CA:       *Centesimus Annus* (Pope John Paul II, 1991).

CCC:      Catechism of the Catholic Church (1994).

CSD:      Compendium of the Social Doctrine of the Church
          (Pope John Paul II, 2004).

DCE:      *Deus Caritas Est* (Pope Benedict XVI, 2005).

DD:       *Dies Domini* (Pope John Paul II, 1998).

DEV:      *Dominum et Vivificantem* (Pope John Paul II, 1986).

DV:       *Dei Verbum* (Vatican II, 1965).

EDE:      *Ecclesia de Eucharistia* (Pope John Paul II, 2003).

EG:       *Evangelii Gaudium* (Pope Francis, 2013).

GS:       *Gaudium et Spes* (Vatican II, 1965).

LF:       *Lumen Fidei* (Pope Francis, 2013).

LG:       *Lumen Gentium* (Vatican II, 1964).

MM:       *Mater et Magistra* (Pope John XXIII, 1961)

MV:       *Misericordiae Vultus* (Pope Francis, 2015).

RM:       *Redemptoris Mater* (Pope John Paul II, 1987).

RN:       *Rerum Novarum* (Pope Leo XIII, 1891).

SC:       *Sacramentum Caritatis* (Pope Benedict XVI, 2007).

USCCA:    US Catholic Catechism for Adults (1994).

VD:       *Verbum Domini* (Pope Benedict XVI, 2010).

Sacred space is a concept that is familiar to most Catholics. When we enter a church, it is instinctive for many of us to kneel or bow or go to the holy water font to bless ourselves because this space is different from all other kinds of places. We know that we have entered God's house. The space is made holy because God is there.

Another type of sacred space is the places made holy by the presence of Jesus while he lived on earth. Pilgrimages to these places are part of Christian piety because they are unique encounters that bridge the life of Jesus while he lived on earth with the living Christ, who remains present to us through the power of the Holy Spirit. The Upper Room on Mount Zion in Jerusalem is one of these very special sacred places.

In *Meeting God in the Upper Room: Three Moments to Change Your Life,* Monsignor Peter Vaghi weaves the events of the Upper Room into a pattern of discipleship that enables us to have a deeper appreciation for Jesus's love for us and for our own call to discipleship. It was in the Upper Room that Jesus celebrated the Last Supper with his disciples and demonstrated the self-giving nature of Christian love. It was in the Upper Room where the Holy Spirit descended upon the apostles and, through that grace, the Church was born. It was from the Upper Room that the apostles became missionaries, emboldened to take the Good News to the ends of the earth. Because Our Lord remains present with us, the Upper Room is not simply a historical location; it becomes an "an icon of the fruitful Church and its fruitfulness continues in and through each and every believer" (107).

At the canonization Mass of St. Junípero Serra, our Holy Father reminded us that "we are heirs to the bold missionary spirit of so many men and women who preferred not to be 'shut up within structures which give us a false sense of security…within habits which make us feel safe, while at our door people are starving' (*EG* 49). We are indebted to a tradition, a chain of witnesses who have made it possible for the good news of the Gospel to be, in every generation, both 'good' and 'news'" (Holy Mass and Canonization of Blessed Father Junípero Serra).

Pope Francis is calling each one of us to live as missionary disciples. Like the apostles who were sent forth from the Upper Room out into the world, each week, each one of us is sent forth from our parish church to the world to be witnesses to Jesus's saving love. Pope Francis writes "every Christian is challenged, here and now, to be actively engaged in evangelization; indeed, anyone who has truly experienced God's saving love does not need much time or lengthy training to go out and proclaim that love" (*EG* 120).

While one may not need lengthy training, the believer needs to ask, "How do I manifest that belief that I am a true disciple of Jesus, that he's risen and walks with me?" With the voice of an experienced and wise preacher and teacher, Monsignor Vaghi helps us answer this question by capturing the lessons of discipleship learned in the school of the Upper Room. We find Jesus and his disciples at prayer, we see Jesus teaching us the nature of self-giving love, we encounter Thomas's doubt turned to faith, and we recognize Mary, Mother of God, becoming Mother of the Church. We learn that in prayer, in the study of God's Word, in active participation in the Mass, in the sharing of our love with those entrusted to us and those most in need of God's love, we manifest Christ's love. By the grace of the sacraments that have their origin in the Upper Room—Eucharist, confirmation, reconciliation, and holy orders—we experience how Jesus uses the sacraments to share his divine life with each one of us and with the world.

As each follower of Jesus recognizes the call to be an evangelizing disciple, we take on the responsibility of renewing our faith, of standing firm in the conviction of its truth and finally of sharing it. Monsignor Vaghi provides guidance and support for all three of those elements in the life of the Christian today who truly wants to take on the mission that came to life in the Upper Room. We should all be grateful to Monsignor Vaghi for offering us this opportunity to spiritually visit the Upper Room and draw strength and inspiration from our encounter with God in that sacred space.

Cardinal Donald Wuerl
Archbishop of Washington

# THE MOST IMPORTANT ROOM IN CHRISTENDOM

## THE CENACLE, THEN AND NOW

The Upper Room, also known as the Cenacle, is located in the southern part of the Old City of Jerusalem on Mount Zion, and is perhaps best known as the traditional site of the Last Supper since the fourth century AD. The current structure of the room dates approximately from the fourteenth century, which accounts for the existing Gothic-era columns.

According to tradition, this is where the apostles stayed when they were in Jerusalem. It is where the Last Supper took place. The Cenacle is where Jesus washed his disciples' feet (John 13:1–20), which symbolizes the ministry of loving service. It is where the concept of a loving friendship with Jesus was introduced, as set forth in John's Last Supper discourses (John 14—16), and gave the apostles a glimpse into the beautiful prayer life of Jesus, sometimes known as the "high priestly prayer," recorded in John 17. It is the place where the disciples gathered in fear after the death of Jesus and prayed, with Mary, for the coming of the Holy Spirit (John 20:19–23).

By tradition, this is same room where Jesus appeared, both before and after the resurrection. It was here that the Risen One made visible his wounds to see and touch, and the room where the faith of Thomas emerged. It is where the Risen Lord breathed on them the Holy Spirit "on the evening of that first day of the week" (John 20:19). It is where tongues of fire appeared to them on Pentecost and "they were all filled with the holy Spirit" (Acts 2:4). That event marks the birthday of the Church in the presence of our Blessed Mother (Acts 1:14). It is from there that the apostles went forth with boldness sharing the Good News.

For all these reasons, the Upper Room is a much sought-after destination for Christians who travel on pilgrimage to the Holy Land. And yet, because it also has great spiritual significance for both Jews and Muslims, the Cenacle is ever at the center of political controversy. Normally only "visits" are allowed to this place because this present structure is contested and claimed by both Israelis and Muslims. Muslims consider it to be a mosque and the Israelis consider the lower level of this structure to be the Tomb of David, which has belonged to the Israelis since 1948. On some occasions, Christians are permitted to celebrate Mass in the Upper Room, but it is not common and is done only with permission.

Even so, the importance of this holy space never ends. In May 2014, Pope Francis visited the Holy Land and was permitted to celebrate Mass in the Cenacle during his three-day pilgrimage. As if to acknowledge this privilege, the pope in his homily said: "It is a great gift that the Lord has given us by bringing us together here in the Upper Room for the celebration of the Eucharist" (May 26, 2014).

Perhaps it is because the apostles spent so much time with Christ in that holy place that we see most clearly their various personalities when they are gathered here, particularly at the Last Supper. Tellingly, it was here that Jesus predicted Judas's betrayal and Peter's denial (John 13:21–30, 36–38), and here exposed Thomas's doubt (John 20:24–29). The humanity of each apostle is vibrantly portrayed in the Upper Room, giving us a glimpse into our own hearts and nature, as well as into the unrelenting love of Jesus Christ for his followers. It was also in this room from which, filled with the Holy Spirit, the apostles would ultimately leave to change the world—your world and mine. For as we hear in Psalm 104:30: "Send forth your spirit, they are created, / and you renew the face of the earth."

Despite the tensions over its religious significance, the events that took place in the Upper Room prior to and immediately after the crucifixion of Christ, and in the days following his Resurrection, can never be undone or forgotten. The fruits of Jesus's life and ministry, as witnessed in the precious moments in the Upper Room documented in Scripture, continue in and through the Church. In this humble space, the most important room in all of Christendom, where Jesus set a remarkable precedent of faith and service, we were given a new understanding of God's love and the revolutionary power of the Holy Spirit was unleashed.

## ENCOUNTERING GOD IN OUR UPPER ROOM

My appreciation for the importance of this holy space, considered by some to be the first Christian church, began with a pilgrimage I led to the Holy Land a number of years ago. Our time in that room made a significant impression on me and on all of my pilgrims. In fact, the origin of this book can be traced to that extraordinary pilgrimage of faith.

And yet, one need not physically go to the Cenacle to be aware of its spiritual importance. What happened in that Upper Room in Jerusalem almost two millennia ago, both before and after Christ's resurrection, continues to have significant and grace-filled personal effects on every baptized Christian. The events that took place there continue to rest at the heart of our faith today.

While the Cenacle is a real place, it is also so much more than a simple room or a concrete historical location in Jerusalem. It is here that the apostles retreated from the world to be with Jesus, here they listened with rapt attention as he revealed to them the mysteries that they would one day pass on to thousands of others. It was here, above all, that they were equipped to do the work for which they had been called.

And in that sense, one need not travel to the Holy Land to encounter Christ. Inside each of us is an "upper room," where we experience the living presence of God. Wherever we are, whenever we take the time to find and speak and listen to God, we can experience his life-giving, sacramental, and transformative presence.

As we ponder what happened out of love for us in that Upper Room at Jerusalem, we begin to experience that this room is an icon of the Church itself. The graces that originated in the events associated with that sacred place continue to transform us through the life of the Church today, creating for us a spiritual home where souls are welcomed and nurtured. My hope in writing this book is to help you be in touch again and again with our God who lives and moves in our very midst, the God of the Upper Room. Just like the apostles, each one of us needs to spend some time in the upper room in our own hearts, drawing close to God in prayer.

I am writing this book from such a place in my own home, where I sleep, work, write, and pray. Your upper room might be in your office, your car, or a quiet nook in your house, a place where God speaks to you anew each day. Others experience these Upper Room moments at Mass, or in Eucharistic Adoration.

As we journey together in this book to experience the events associated with that original Upper Room, we will be introduced (or reintroduced) to the unique atmosphere of that Cenacle in Jerusalem in some detail. In doing so, my prayer is that you might experience a renewed sense of God's presence in your life, and the graces he wants to pour out upon you that can be traced to the events that transpired in that holy place. The graces that originate from that sacred space continue and are at the heart of our living faith today.

## THREE EVENTS IN THE UPPER ROOM

In that Upper Room during his 2014 visit to Jerusalem, Pope Francis's homily highlighted three major events that took place in that sacred space: "Here, where Jesus shared the Last Supper with the apostles; where, after his resurrection, he appeared in their midst; where the Holy Spirit descended with power upon Mary and the disciples, here the Church was born, and she was born *to go forth*."[1]

And so, following the pope's teaching, I have divided this book into three parts:

• The Last Supper

• The post-Resurrection appearances of the Risen Lord

• Pentecost and its effects on the apostles and early Church

From our perspective almost two millennia later, in these three points in history we see an image of a fruitful Church in that room and from that room. The life of our Church today continues to be reflective of what happened there.

## EXPERIENCING THE LIFE OF THE CHURCH

The events in the Upper Room reveal a great deal about the way we experience the life of the Church. We experience that life…

*In sacramental graces.* In the Upper Room, Jesus instituted three specific sacraments—the Eucharist, holy orders, and penance. A fourth sacrament (confirmation) has its origin in the imposition of hands that, in a certain way, perpetuates the grace of Pentecost that took place in the Upper Room by the coming of the Holy Spirit. The graces from these sacraments continue to strengthen and sustain the Church in every age.

*In service.* In the washing of feet on Holy Thursday, we catch a glimpse of the "servant leadership" Christ taught his disciples to practice. "But Jesus summoned them and said, 'You know that the rulers of the Gentiles lord it over them.... But it shall not be so among you. Rather, whoever wishes to be great among you shall be your servant; whoever wishes to be first among you shall be your slave'" (Matthew 20:25–27).

*In prayer.* In his high priestly prayer, Jesus prayed not only for his immediate followers but for all those who would follow: "I pray not only for them, but also for those who will believe in me through their word, so that they may all be one, as you, Father, are in me and I in you, that they also may be in us, that the world may believe that you sent me" (John 17:20–21).

*In the profession of Easter faith.* As the darkness of Good Friday gives way to the jubilant "Alleluia" of Easter, we profess our faith with all the joy of St. Thomas in seeing the Risen Lord. "My Lord and my God!" (John 20:28).

*In the outpouring of the gifts of the Spirit.* In the sacraments, particularly at baptism and again at confirmation, the scent of chrism fills our senses with inexplicable joy, just as the followers of Jesus were overwhelmed by the coming of the Holy Spirit at Pentecost. Listen to Peter, as he proclaims the fulfillment of Joel's prophecy: "'It will come to pass in the last days,' God says, 'that I will pour out a portion of my spirit upon all flesh...and it shall be that everyone shall be saved who calls on the name of the Lord'" (Acts 2:17, 21).

*In the presence of Mary.* Quitting that Upper Room and following her Son as closely as possible, sharing in his suffering as only a mother could, Mary is the icon of Mother Church. Listen as Jesus speaks to her and the "beloved disciple" from the cross: "When Jesus saw his mother and the disciple there whom he loved, he said to his mother, 'Woman, behold, your son.' Then he said to the disciple, 'Behold, your mother.' And from that hour the disciple took her into his home" (John 19:26–27).

*In apostolic zeal.* The fire that fell at Pentecost did not remain in that Upper Room, but continued to sustain the missionary nature of the Church to the present day. As Paul and Barnabas proclaimed the Gospel to the Gentiles: "For so the Lord has commanded us, 'I have made you a light to the Gentiles, that you may be an instrument of salvation to the ends of the earth'" (Acts 13:47).

As Pope Francis said, speaking from the Cenacle on May 26, 2014: "How much love and goodness has flowed from the Upper Room! How much charity has gone forth from here, like a river from its source, beginning as a stream and then expanding and becoming a great torrent. All the saints drew from this source; and hence the great river of the Church's holiness continues to flow: from the heart of Christ, from the Eucharist and from the Holy Spirit."[2]

# PART ONE

# THE UPPER ROOM—THE LAST SUPPER

Leonardo Da Vinci, *The Last Supper,* 1498.
Convent of Santa Maria delle Grazie, Milan, Italy.

The first major event in the Upper Room was the Last Supper. How important it is to spend some time pondering the preparation for that meal and the significance of that meal! It was Jesus's final meal with his twelve apostles on the night before he died. There was a familial intimacy there as these apostles had travelled together during Jesus's public life in the last three years and they knew each other well. It was at this final meal on the occasion of the Passover that Jesus gave them the assurance and the graces they would need to carry on their mission after his death.

For us, this event takes on profound significance as well. Once we catch a glimpse of the events that transpired in this room, we will be forever captivated by the mystery of the God who loves us so much that, even as he prepared to return to the Father, promised that "I will not leave you orphaned; I am coming to you" (John 14:18, NRSV).

# CHAPTER ONE

# Finding the Room

### *Preparing for the Last Supper and for the Mass Today*

On the first day of the Feast of Unleavened Bread, the disciples
approached Jesus and said, "Where do you want us to prepare for
you to eat the Passover?" he said, "Go into the city to a certain man
and tell him, 'The teacher says, "My appointed time draws near; in
your house I shall celebrate the Passover with my disciples.""" The
disciples then did as Jesus had ordered, and prepared the Passover.

—Matthew 26:17–19

## The Details of Preparation

In all three synoptic Gospels (Matthew, Mark, and Luke), we read that
Jesus anticipated the Passover meal as he arrived in Jerusalem, and
understood the need to prepare for it. The careful and varying details
in each of the accounts give weight to the importance of what was to
happen there.

The Upper Room was very much on his mind. In Matthew's Gospel,
Jesus gives his disciples specific instructions about how they were to
prepare for the event, though they could not have known how significant that evening would be for them all—the last time Jesus would
celebrate with them in this world. As we read the other Gospel narra-
tives, even the smallest details take on eternal significance. Reading
Mark's Gospel, we see that Jesus was more specific, even prophetic
about the details:

> He sent two of his disciples and said to them, "Go into the city and
> a man will meet you, *carrying a jar of water. Follow him.* Wherever he
> enters, say to the master of the house, 'The Teacher says, "Where is
> my guest room where I may eat the Passover with my disciples?"'

Then *he will show you a large upper room furnished and ready.* Make the preparations for us there." The disciples then went off, entered the city, and found it just as he had told them; and they prepared the Passover (Mark 14:13–16).

Jesus is even more detailed and prophetic in the account of Luke.

When the day of the feast of Unleavened Bread arrived, the day for sacrificing the Passover lamb, he sent out Peter and John, instructing them, "Go and make preparations for us to eat the Passover." They asked him, "Where do you want us to make the preparations?" And he answered them, *"When you go into the city, a man will meet you* carrying a jar of water. *Follow him into the house* that he enters and say to the master of the house, 'The teacher says to you, "Where is the guest room where I may eat the Passover with my disciples?"' he will show you a large upper room that is furnished. Make the preparations there." *Then they went off and found everything exactly as he had told them,* and there they prepared the Passover (Luke 22:7–13).

The nuances of each Gospel account vary, as often do the details of the same story between different storytellers. Yet we consistently see the importance of the room reflected in Jesus's words. In all three accounts, it is clear that he has a specific place in mind. The room itself is a part of God's plan, a designated holy space that is ready and waiting to receive Jesus and all that is to come.

## AN EAGER DESIRE

And when the "Hour" came, Jesus took his place at table in the Upper Room with his apostles, the Upper Room which had been prepared, and said to them: *"I have eagerly desired to eat this Passover with you before I suffer* for, I tell you, I shall not eat it again until there is fulfillment in the kingdom of God" (Luke 22:15–16).

The words "eagerly desired" are unique to the Gospel account of St. Luke. Here, we get a taste of God's longing for relationship with his followers. These two words, so easy to miss in a quick reading, are just a spark in the flame of Jesus's love for his disciples. Knowing all that was to come—knowing even then that one of the men in that very room would betray him—Jesus still "eagerly desired" to share a meal with them. He stands before them and offers his unconditional friendship, eagerly inviting them to share the Passover with him.

In the book of Revelation, we find a powerful image of the Lord who knocks on the door of our hearts, and waits to be welcomed inside: "Behold, I stand at the door and knock. If anyone hears my voice and opens the door, I will enter his house and dine with him, and he with me" (Revelation 3:20).

In our day, Jesus knocks at the door of our hearts and eagerly desires to dine with us at the sacrificial meal we call the Eucharist. He wishes to find us ready to receive him, to sit down and eat with him, in the upper rooms of our lives.

How urgently do we respond to his request? Do we "eagerly desire" to be with him, too? Do we prepare our hearts to respond each Sunday and holy day? During the weekdays? Occasionally? Periodically?

In the *Catechism of the Catholic Church,* we read: "As often as the sacrifice of the Cross…is celebrated on the altar, the work of our redemption is carried out" (*CCC* 1364). Read those words again, and let them sink into your heart and take root there. What a profound way to think about the Eucharist! How can we not eagerly desire to participate in the Eucharist if we understand that our salvation, our very redemption is at stake?

### Preparing Your Upper Room

Returning to the Gospel text, the apostles obey Jesus's command and see to it that the Upper Room is set for the Passover meal. Jesus was quite explicit in his instructions in all three of the synoptic Gospels, and the disciples carefully obeyed.

So much was in store for the apostles, much more than they possibly could have anticipated. They had no idea that it was their last meal together, or how much they would learn and experience at that meal. All they knew is what their Master told them. All they could do was follow his instructions.

How do we prepare ourselves for the Eucharist? Our preparations are different than the preparations required of the disciples for the Last Supper. They were concerned about finding the right room in Jerusalem, the room Jesus directed them to find.

For us, there is an internal preparation that is required. Worthy preparation is essential. But what does that mean to prepare worthily for participation in the Eucharist? It is Jesus Christ, after all, we receive at Holy Communion. It is his revealed Word that we hear in the Gospel each time we gather.

The *United States Catechism for Adults* clearly states that we need to prepare ourselves for reception of our Lord in Holy Communion. That preparation includes the following:

*Go to confession if needed.* We must be in a state of grace, without any awareness of having committed a serious sin. If we have committed a grave or serious sin, we must go to confession before receiving the sacrament (*USCCA* 222).

*Don't forget to fast!* We are to refrain from eating or drinking anything except water or medicine for at least one hour prior to receiving Holy Communion (*USCCA* 222).

*Let your interior reverence guide your actions.* The *Catechism of the Catholic Church* adds: "Bodily demeanor (gestures, clothing) ought to convey the respect, solemnity and joy of this moment when Christ becomes our guest" (*CCC* 1387). It is, after all, God's house and we are his guests.

*Reflect on the readings before Mass, if possible.* This can be especially helpful if you or members of your household (children especially) have difficulty following the readings or the homily. Take time before Mass to read, study, and ponder that week's Scripture texts. These are easily found online, or in your parish missal. Just as one would not normally attend an opera without studying the libretto, it is all the more important and helpful to read and pray over the Word of God before hearing it proclaimed at Mass, or listening to the priest or deacon reflect upon the readings during the homily.

*Come a little early if you can, and remain for the entire liturgy.* Arriving at Mass prior to the posted time helps us place ourselves in the proper disposition to appropriate fully the sacred mysteries, and to avail ourselves of the graces the Lord is waiting to pour out upon us.

*Don't forget to visit Jesus during the week!* Eucharistic Adoration outside of the Mass is another wonderful means to prepare for Mass. In his Post-Synodal Apostolic Exhortation, *Sacramentum Caritatis*, Pope Benedict XVI writes:

> The act of adoration outside Mass prolongs and intensifies all that takes place during the liturgical celebration itself. Indeed, "only in adoration can a profound and genuine reception mature. And it is precisely this personal encounter with the Lord that then strengthens the social mission contained in the Eucharist, which seeks to break down not only the walls that separate the Lord and ourselves, but also and especially the walls that separate us from one another" (*SC* 66).

The disciples, under the direction of Jesus himself, prepared for the Last Supper by finding the specific space in the Upper Room at Jerusalem. For us, another type of preparation is required. It is a spiritual and personal preparation. Both forms of preparation, space and spiritual, are necessary for a proper and fruitful celebration of the Eucharist. By taking time to prepare our hearts in this way before going to Mass, we often find that the seed of God's Word takes deeper root in us, assisting us in living his Word more fully in daily life.

# CHAPTER TWO

# JESUS INSTITUTES TWO SACRAMENTS— EUCHARIST AND HOLY ORDERS

The LORD said to Moses and Aaron…: For on this same night I will
go through Egypt, striking down every firstborn in the land, human
being and beast alike, and executing judgment on all the gods of
Egypt—I, the LORD! But for you the blood will mark the houses
where you are. Seeing the blood, I will pass over you; thereby, when
I strike the land of Egypt, no destructive blow will come upon you.

—Exodus 12:1, 12–13

## THE HISTORY BEHIND THE MEAL

It was in the context of the Jewish Passover meal that Jesus celebrated
the Last Supper with his apostles and instituted the Eucharist in the
Upper Room. The Last Supper has important roots in the Jewish experience of the Passover and Passover meal. For the Jewish people, this
annual celebration, called "a perpetual institution," commemorates
their emancipation from slavery by the Egyptians. Scripture details
explicitly what they were to do in preparing that meal.

According to the detailed instructions found in Exodus 12, Jews
were to slaughter a young lamb and apply some of the blood from the
lamb on the two doorposts and the lintel of every house in which they
celebrated the meal. For the Israelites who were enslaved in Egypt at
the time, the blood was a sign to the Lord to *pass over* the firstborn in
their homes. Homes without the mark of the lamb fell victim to the
Tenth Plague, the death of the firstborn.

Thus, the name Passover is derived. The importance of this event was
so significant that the Lord commanded the Jews to remember it: "This

day will be a day of remembrance for you, which your future generations will celebrate with pilgrimage to the LORD; you will celebrate it
as a statute forever" (Exodus 12:14).

Certainly Jesus knew the significance of the Passover in preparation for the Last Supper, and the symbolism of the meal is monumental
in the sacrament of the Eucharist, which he instituted in the Upper
Room. That action by Jesus, on the night before he died, was one of the
defining moments in the Upper Room for all times. Its effects continue
each and every time we gather for Eucharist. As Pope Benedict XVI
said, "In the sacrament of the altar, the Lord meets us, men and women
created in God's image and likeness (cf. Genesis 1:27), and becomes
our companion along the way. In this sacrament, the Lord truly becomes
food for us, to satisfy our hunger for truth and freedom. Since only the
truth can make us free (cf. John 8:32), Christ becomes for us the food
of truth" (SC 2).

That night, Jesus broke bread with his disciples and forever altered
the relationship between God and humankind. He is the bread of life
broken for you and me and pledge of the life to come.

### THE INSTITUTION OF THE EUCHARIST

Writing about the institution of the Eucharist at the Last Supper in his
book *Jesus of Nazareth: Holy Week*, Pope Benedict XVI describes the ritual
as a "foundational event" in the lives of the Jewish people, marking their
deliverance as slaves:

> This ritual meal, which called for the sacrifice of lambs (cf. Exodus
> 12:1–28, 43–51), was a remembrance of the past, but at the same
> time a prophetic remembrance, the proclamation of a deliverance
> yet to come…. This is the context in which Jesus introduces the
> newness of his gift. In the prayer of praise, the *Berakah*, he does
> not simply thank the Father for the great events of past history,

but also for his own "exaltation." In instituting the sacrament of the Eucharist, Jesus anticipates and makes present the sacrifice of the cross and the victory of the resurrection. At the same time, he reveals that he himself is the *true* sacrificial lamb, destined in the Father's plan from the foundation of the world.... The institution of the Eucharist demonstrates how Jesus' death, for all its violence and absurdity, became in him a supreme act of love and mankind's definitive deliverance from evil." (*SC* 10) "Jesus' Last Supper—which includes not only a prophecy, but a real anticipation of the Cross and Resurrection in the Eucharistic gifts—was regarded as a Passover: as his Passover."[3]

There are four scriptural accounts of the institution narrative of the Eucharist at the Last Supper in the Upper Room—provided by Matthew, Mark, Luke, and Paul's First Letter to the Corinthians. They are all similar in essentials, leaving us to meditate upon the details.

> While they were eating, Jesus took bread, said the blessing, broke it, and giving it to his disciples said, "Take and eat; this is my body." Then he took a cup, gave thanks, and gave it to them, saying, "Drink from it, all of you, for this is my blood of the covenant, which will be shed on behalf of many for the forgiveness of sins. I tell you, from now on I shall not drink this fruit of the vine until the day when I drink it with you new in the kingdom of my Father." (Matthew 26:26–29)

The Pauline account, written around AD 56, is the oldest in literary terms. Though Paul was not present at the Last Supper, his account reflects the same precision of language used in the three Gospel texts:

> For I received from the Lord what I also handed on to you, that the Lord Jesus, on the night he was handed over, took bread, and, after he had given thanks, broke it and said, "This is my body that is for

you. Do this in remembrance of me." In the same way also the cup, after supper, saying, "This cup is the new covenant in my blood. Do this, as often as you drink it, in remembrance of me." (1 Corinthians 11:23–25)

Pope Benedict XVI writes, "From the point of view of historical evidence, nothing could be more authentic than this Last Supper tradition."[4] The words of Christ on the night before he died—repeated in Matthew, Mark, Luke, and Acts—instituted the sacrament of the Eucharist. In so doing, he sought "to perpetuate the sacrifice of the cross (that what he was about to endure out of his incredible love for each of us) throughout the ages until he should come again…" (*CCC* 1323). He commands his apostles to "do this in memory of me." His words are not a passive sentimentality. No, Jesus's words were a call to action; they were a command: *"Do this* in memory of me." In the words of Pope Benedict XVI in his encyclical *Deus Caritas Est*: "Love can be 'commanded' because it has first been given" (*DCE* 14).

Those many years ago in Jerusalem, Jesus and his disciples gathered to share a historic meal. The sacrament of the Eucharist, the greatest gift and mystery given to us throughout the ages, was instituted in a quiet moment between Jesus and those dearest to him. And that history continues in our day. It is as if each one of us were sitting in that Upper Room with the twelve apostles every time we celebrate the Eucharist. The same words that reverberated throughout the Upper Room millennia ago are heard by us over and over again, in our churches every day, at each and every moment of the day, somewhere in this world of ours.

## The Institution of Holy Orders

Another important sacrament was initiated that night. In ordering his disciples to "Do this in memory of me," he not only instituted the Eucharist, he made the apostles his first priests. Two sacraments: Eucharist and Holy Orders. Two great, lasting gifts of the Upper Room.

The *Catechism* tells us: "The Eucharist that Christ institutes at that moment will be the memorial of his sacrifice. Jesus includes the apostles in his own offering and bids them perpetuate it. By doing so, the Lord institutes his apostles as priests of the New Covenant: 'For their sakes I sanctify myself, so that they also may be sanctified in truth'" (*CCC* 611).

From that very room and because of what happened there, generations of priests throughout the centuries have been born. Every priest is defined by doing what Jesus commanded at that meal—to do this in the Lord's memory.

### The Implication of What Happened That Night

The command may seem simple, but "remembering" Jesus, and especially what God has done for us on the cross, is much more than the ability to recall a story or share it as an experience. The supreme act of love in which Jesus died, that which we remember each time we celebrate the Eucharist, actually brings us into an intimacy with him at a most profound level. There is no conceivable way to deepen our friendship, our knowledge and love of Jesus, and his love for us, than through the celebration of the most holy Eucharist. It is thus "the source and summit of our lives" as followers of Jesus (*CCC* 1324).

In the words of Pope Francis, "The Lord in the Eucharist makes us follow his path, that of service, of sharing, of giving—and what little we have, what little we are, if shared, becomes wealth, because the power of God, which is that of love, descends into our poverty to transform it. Let us ask ourselves…do I let myself be transformed by him? Do I let the Lord who gives himself to me, guide me to come out more and more from my little fence, to get out and be not afraid to give, to share, to love him and others?"[5]

The Eucharist calls us all to this transformation, priest and layperson alike. If we do this, then what was initiated in that Upper Room millennia ago becomes not simply a one-time experience but a pronounced way of life destined to change the world and each one of us in the process. The words are simple, yes. But the command has eternal significance: "Do this in memory of me" (Luke 22:19).

There is an inseparable link between the Eucharist and Holy Orders—these two wonderful gifts of the Lord Jesus from the Upper Room. At the altar, the priest reminds us daily of Christ's ultimate act of love for us on the cross and through what happened with his apostles in the Upper Room at that last supper. There could be no greater gift from our Lord Jesus than the privilege and vocation of the priesthood—this service for his holy people.

By the power of the Holy Spirit, the priest prays the words of consecration at every Mass—in the person of Christ— "Make holy, therefore, these gifts, we pray, by sending down your Spirit upon them like the dewfall, so that they may become for us the Body and Blood of our Lord Jesus Christ." As such, without the priest, there can be no Eucharist—this bread of life and cup of eternal salvation. It is at once the priest's most unique privilege and obligation—the celebration of the Eucharist, which is the source and summit of our lives as Catholic Christians. The priesthood and the Eucharist are thus truly lasting legacies of the Upper Room.

## From History into Eternity

The Upper Room at Jerusalem was reserved for Jesus and the twelve apostles on the night before he died. There was not much room for anyone else that night; the room was small and the crowd gathered comprised Jesus's most intimate friends. Since that time, however, there have been more and more seats added to the table of "upper rooms" throughout the world.

This additional seating is, in the words of Pope Benedict XVI, a revolution of sorts. In his Corpus Christi homily in 2008, he said: "The deepest (most profound) revolution of human history…is experienced precisely gathered around the Eucharist. Here people of different ages, sex, social condition and political ideas gather…. We open ourselves to each other to become one in him."[6]

In this revolution, we uniquely experience the sacrament of love. For no greater love exists than to lay down one's life for one's friends. And that is precisely what Jesus did for us. The revolution he started is what we celebrate and reenact every time we gather for this sacrament of love.

At every Mass, the Eucharist draws us into Jesus's act of self-offering. This dynamic and intimate encounter happens, according to St. John Paul II in his encyclical *Ecclesia de Eucharistia,* "through a real contact, since this sacrifice is made present ever anew, sacramentally perpetuated…. What is repeated is its memorial celebration…which makes Christ's one, definitive redemptive sacrifice always present in time" (*EDE* 12). We know that "the ordained priest in the Mass links the Eucharistic consecration to the sacrifice of the Cross and to the Last Supper, thus making it possible that the sacrifice of Christ becomes the sacrifice of all the members of the Church…. This also reminds us of the importance of sacrifice in each individual's life" (*USCCA* 221). What a profound mystery!

In the Eucharist, we actually receive the Risen Jesus—an encounter that transforms and miraculously changes us into him. We experience the Love that is his very Person. "For my flesh is true food and my blood is true drink. Whoever eats my flesh and drinks my blood remains in me, and I in him" (John 6:55–56). This is a revolutionary promise from the revealed words of Jesus himself!

Of course, we should not be surprised. St. Augustine reminds us that we "become Who it is that [we] receive." Since the Eucharist is the bread of life, it is Jesus, "the living bread." Jesus actually transforms us into himself in the Eucharist. We become his living body. We become the Church precisely each time we eat of his body and drink his blood. "Because the loaf of bread is one, we, though many, are one body, for we all partake of the one loaf" (1 Corinthians 10:17). We become one body.

This happens in the Eucharist when Christ offers his Body and Blood as food under the signs of bread and wine. The bread we eat and the cup we drink is truly Jesus Christ. Yes, it is Jesus. It is his real presence. He is present to us in many ways. The Eucharist is his most powerful and intense presence. It is always worthwhile, especially in adoration before the Blessed Sacrament, to spend some time meditating and focusing on what truly happens at the Eucharist.

The Church continually calls and challenges us to reflect on the central role of the Eucharist in Catholic life. Through the sacrament, we are stepping out of history and into the eternal moment in which Jesus became the Passover Lamb on our behalf.

## Preparing Your Upper Room

The perennial challenge of our Church is to recoup a sense of the sacred, especially in the presence of the Blessed Sacrament. A simple act of genuflection or a reverent bow before the Blessed Sacrament is an expression of deep respect and love for the Lord Jesus. Jesus, in the Blessed Sacrament, is, after all, the principal mystery of our faith. Remember, "Jesus thus brings his own radical *novum* to the ancient Hebrew sacrificial meal.... The ancient rite has been brought to fulfillment and definitively surpassed by the loving gift of the incarnate Son of God" (*SC* 11). Could there be a more profound mystery?

Could there be a more powerful contact, after all, with the living God than his own Body and Blood, the eating of his very Body and the drinking of his very Blood?

It is Jesus's very self-gift, his sacrificial love for us, his dying and rising out of love for us, that we celebrate at each and every Mass, every Eucharist, *this* commemoration, *this* memorial (*this* making present of a past event), *this* reenactment of his death on Calvary and his glorious resurrection, *this* memorial of his wonderful love for us.

In the Eucharist "we [actually] enter into the very dynamic of *his* self-giving" (*SC* 11). In addition, "the Eucharist draws us into Jesus' act of self-oblation. More than just statically receiving the incarnate . . . Jesus 'draws us into himself'" (*SC* 11).

At every Mass, this happens "through a real contact, since *this sacrifice is made present ever anew,* sacramentally perpetuated" (*EDE* 12). We know that "What is repeated is its memorial celebration . . . which makes Christ's one, definitive redemptive sacrifice always present in time" (*EDE* 12). Furthermore, we know that "The ordained priest in the Mass links the Eucharistic consecration to the sacrifice of the Cross and to the Last Supper, thus making it possible that the sacrifice of Christ becomes the sacrifice of all the members of the Church. . . . This also reminds us of the importance of sacrifice in each individual's life" (*USCCA* 221).

What a profound mystery!

In this chapter we considered briefly the two gifts of the Upper Room, the gifts of Eucharist and of Holy Orders. As you take time to withdraw into your own upper room, ask yourself: How have these two sacraments been gifts to you, in your own spiritual journey, and within your own vocation?

# CHAPTER THREE

# A Closer Look at the Personalities at the Last Supper

When he had said this, Jesus was deeply troubled and testified, "Amen, amen, I say to you, one of you will betray me." The disciples looked at one another, at a loss as to whom he meant.

—John 13:21–22

## Conversation Clusters

One of the most famous artistic portrayals of the Upper Room is the late fifteenth-century masterpiece by Leonardo da Vinci titled *The Last Supper*. Appropriately, it was painted on the walls of the refectory (dining hall) of the convent of Santa Maria delle Grazie in Milano, Italy.

In viewing this masterpiece on a recent visit, I was struck by the four groupings of three apostles, each positioned around the table with Jesus in the center. In today's parlance, we would refer to these as "conversation clusters." The painting seems to depict the different reactions of the disciples in the charged moment immediately following Jesus's prediction that one of them would betray him.[7]

Providentially, as I focused on the masterpiece, it struck me that the three personalities I had chosen to focus on in this chapter were part of the same cluster—Peter, John, and Judas—next to Jesus on his right. These three personalities reflect denial, love, and betrayal. Each one of us can relate to these personalities at some point in our lives. What happened in the Upper Room involving these three apostles is a model for each of us.

## A Gathering (and Argument) Among Friends

As reflected in the artistic rendering of Da Vinci, it is clear that the Last Supper was what might be called an "invitation only" gathering. I am sure the apostles had no idea that it would be their last meal together with Jesus. Most likely they were enjoying the Passover celebration together as they had before—as a gathering of friends.

Arms outstretched, at the center of the table, is Jesus. His position in Da Vinci's painting signifies what we know to be true. He was the most important personality at table. It was his gathering, and was something truly unique. It may have started off feeling like a typical gathering to the apostles, but Jesus's next words may have caused a few of them to sense the weight of the moment: "I have eagerly desired to eat this Passover with you before I suffer, for I tell you, I shall not eat it again until there is fulfillment in the kingdom of God" (Luke 22:15–16).

It was much more than a simple Passover meal or even a farewell dinner. Jesus knew in his heart what this meal in the Upper Room was about and what it would forever accomplish. In his book *The Eucharistic Heart,* Jesuit Father Jean Galot writes that the Lord's eager desire to institute the Eucharist that night "is above all the desire for a gift which contains the gift of the passion and which is destined to be multiplied indefinitely for our benefit so as to make the mystery of the death and resurrection part of our lives."[8]

It was clear, however, from the outset that the apostles—those privileged personalities around the table with Jesus—had other concerns. According to Luke's Gospel, immediately following Jesus's announcement that one of the men at the table would betray him, the disciples fell into an argument that was centered not on Christ, but on their own egos: "Then an argument broke out among them about which of them should be regarded as the greatest" (Luke 22:24). Jesus then had to rebuke them, saying: "…let the greatest among you be as the youngest, and the leader as the servant. For who is greater: the one seated at table or the one who serves…I am among you as the one who serves" (Luke 22:26–27).

This notion of service is an important aspect of Jesus's ministry and message in the Upper Room that I will discuss in a later chapter.

What else happened in the Upper Room at table that night involving a few of the personalities? The rest of this chapter will examine the trio in Da Vinci's painting I mentioned earlier: Peter, Judas, and John. That night, Jesus predicted the denial of Peter and the betrayal of Judas. There is the tradition of John being the "beloved" disciple. Denial, betrayal, and love are human qualities that are a part of our earthly condition, qualities that each of us expresses at different times in our lives. These three men, clustered together in conversation in the famous painting, are an image of qualities found in all of us—qualities that were as important to the faith of each disciple as they are in our own lives.

## AN IMAGE OF DENIAL

In Matthew, Mark, Luke, and John, the denial of Peter was foretold at the Last Supper. Initially, Peter is characteristically convinced that his faith is strong. In Luke's Gospel, we see a conversation between Simon Peter and Jesus in which Jesus tells him, "I have prayed that your own faith may not fail." Peter's reaction to this comment is one of certainty: "He said to him, 'Lord, I am prepared to go to prison and to die with you.'" But the Lord predicts that "before the cock crows this day, you will deny three times that you know me" (Luke 22:32–34).

Peter's insistence that his faith will not falter is dogged. In Mark's Gospel text, Peter resists Jesus's prophecy further, saying, "Even though all should have their faith shaken, mine will not be.... Even though I should have to die with you, I will not deny you" (Mark 14:29–31). In John's Gospel, before Jesus predicts Peter's denial, Peter says to him, "I will lay down my life for you" (John 13:37). Peter has not yet come face-to-face with his own weakness, his own limitations. He is so sure that his faith will not fail that it never occurs to him to ask the Lord for strength. How often do we do the same?

We all know what happens. Both of the apostles—Judas as well as Peter—abandon the Lord. In each Gospel, Judas hands over Jesus to his enemies; in each Gospel, we see a frightened Peter thrice deny that he ever knew his Master. We now take a closer look at the Gospel of Mark:

> While Peter was below in the courtyard, one of the high priest's maids came along. Seeing Peter warming himself, she looked intently at him and said, "You too were with the Nazarene, Jesus." But he denied it saying, "I neither know nor understand what you are talking about." So he went out into the outer court. Then the cock crowed. The maid saw him and began again to say to the bystanders, "This man is one of them." Once again he denied it. A little later the bystanders said to Peter once more, "Surely you are one of them; for you too are a Galilean." He began to curse and to swear, "I do not know this man about whom you are talking." And immediately a cock crowed a second time (Mark 14:66–72).

It might be tempting for us to shake our heads at Peter while reading these words, but who among us can honestly say we have never denied Christ? Who has never once struggled with fear or uncertainty? Denial is something with which we are all intimately familiar. And yet, Jesus is merciful. In the words of Pope Francis:

> Let us…remember Peter: three times he denied Jesus, precisely when he should have been closest to him; and when he hits bottom he meets the gaze of Jesus who patiently, wordlessly, says to him: "Peter, don't be afraid of your weakness, trust in Me." Peter understands, he feels the loving gaze of Jesus and he weeps. How beautiful is this gaze of Jesus—how much tenderness is there! Brothers and sisters, let us never lose trust in the patience and mercy of God!"[9]

How can we judge Peter when even the One he denied—Jesus—looks upon him with such tender mercy? The moment Peter hears the rooster crow, he recognizes what he has done and is stricken: "Then Peter remembered the word that Jesus had said to him, 'Before the cock crows twice you will deny me three times.' He broke down and wept" (Mark 14:72). Just as Peter demonstrates our own capacity to deny Christ, he also reflects the emotional moment we experience when we, too, feel the loving gaze of Jesus.

## An Image of Betrayal

As with Peter's story, all four Gospels give an account of the prediction of Judas's betrayal at the Last Supper and the actual betrayal thereafter. In addition, as if to highlight its importance, two of the four Eucharistic prayers in the Roman Missal introduce the words of institution by referring to the betrayal—"For on the night he was betrayed…" (Eucharistic Prayer II) and "At the time he was betrayed…" (Eucharistic Prayer III).

In Peter's story, one can sense the deep compassion in Jesus's words when he predicts Peter's betrayal. Likewise, as Jesus speaks about his betrayer, there is a sense of sorrow: "Deeply troubled, Jesus says, 'And yet behold, the hand of the one who is to betray me is with me on the table…woe to that man by whom he is betrayed'" (Luke 22:21–22).

We know, of course, that the man about whom he was speaking was Judas Iscariot. Judas took the morsel that Jesus dipped, and Jesus acknowledged this action as the signifier of his betrayer. At this point, Judas had already been paid his thirty pieces of silver. He had already agreed to turn his friend and teacher over to the chief priests (Matthew 26:14–16). Perhaps the coins were in his pocket at that moment, heavy against his hip. And yet, Judas—like Peter—denies Jesus's words: "Then Judas, his betrayer, said in reply, 'Surely it is not I, Rabbi?' he answered, 'You have said so'" (Matthew 26:25).

Again, denial. These two men who walked with Jesus, who saw his miracles and believed in his teachings, could not accept the truth he spoke directly to them in the Upper Room. Their instinct was to deny their own brokenness, their own proclivity to sin against their Master. The striking difference between them, however, is this: Peter denies what he *will* do; Judas denies what he has *already* begun to do.

The exchange between Judas and Jesus is both brief and devastating. As soon as Judas takes the morsel from Jesus, Jesus tells him, "What you are going to do, do quickly" (John 13:27). So Judas leaves the Upper Room as "it was night" (John 13:30) and "Satan entered him" (John 13:27). Mere moments after denying that he is the betrayer, Judas turns his back on Jesus and leaves the gathering to finalize arrangements for his friend's arrest. Unlike Peter, who was humbled the moment he heard the cock crow after thrice denying Jesus, Judas slips quickly out the door into the night. He quite literally walks out of the light and into the darkness.

## An Image of Love

John's account speaks of another personality at the table, that of St. John, and the tradition of the "beloved" disciple. In John's Gospel, we see an image of the apostle leaning against Jesus's chest. When Jesus announces he will be betrayed by someone in the room, the Scriptures tell us:

> One of his disciples, the one whom Jesus loved, was reclining at Jesus' side. So Simon Peter nodded to him to find out whom he meant. He leaned back against Jesus' chest and said to him, "Master, who is it?" (John 13:23–24).

Da Vinci's mural depicts John leaning toward Peter, capturing the moment, perhaps, that Peter signaled him to ask Jesus the identity of the betrayer. Both the biblical account and the artistic rendering clearly place John nearest Jesus, representing their deep friendship.

The love John had for Jesus is a powerful thing to witness in the Scripture. John was the only apostle standing beneath the cross as Jesus was being crucified. From the cross, Jesus tells his mother, "Woman, behold, your son." And to John, the beloved disciple, Jesus says, "Behold, your mother" (John 19:26–27). It was John who "saw and believed" that Jesus had risen when he saw the burial cloths of Jesus in the tomb "on the first day of the week" (John 20:1, 8). That moment was his expression of Easter faith.

Have you ever wondered why, out of twelve men, John was the only one to display such unabashed, unhesitating devotion to Jesus? In the same way we might be tempted to judge Peter for thrice denying Jesus, with John, we might be tempted to judge ourselves for lacking his unwavering devotion. Yet neither course is appropriate. John is, indeed, an image of love, and an example of faith that should inspire us. But his love for his Lord is not some unattainable ideal. It is a very real, very human example of the intimate relationship between God and his children. The friendship between Jesus and John is the friendship available to each of us through the Eucharist.

### An Image of Ourselves

What happened among these specific personalities at the table that night has implications for each of us. As we reflect on them more deeply, might we not see ourselves at table in the Upper Room in some way?

In addition to John the beloved (and of course Jesus himself), there were two Upper Room personalities of special focus. The first is Peter who, out of weakness and a seeming lack of courage, would deny Jesus three times. He would ultimately make his profession of faith after the Resurrection when he reassured the Risen Lord of his love. Then Jesus told him, "Feed my sheep" (John 21:17). Jesus invited Peter to follow him.

Peter would become the prince of the apostles, after undoing the denial that Jesus had predicted at the Last Supper with a triple affirmation of love for the Risen Jesus (John 21:15–19). Peter's ministry of unity continues in the Church today, even after these many years. Peter now bears the name of Francis.

It was so different for the second personality at table, for Judas. Matthew's account sets forth the feelings of Judas after the betrayal as one who Jesus wished had never been born (Matthew 26:24). Like Peter, Judas ultimately regrets his sin.

> Then Judas, his betrayer, seeing that Jesus had been condemned, deeply regretted what he had done. He returned the thirty pieces of silver to the chief priests and elders, saying, "I have sinned in betraying innocent blood." They said, "What is that to us? Look to it yourself." Flinging the money into the temple, he departed and went off and hanged himself. (Matthew 27:3–5)

In the end, was it possible that Judas might have experienced a deathbed conversion of heart, similar to that of the thief Dismas on the cross? We will never know for sure. Nothing is impossible with God. Perhaps if Judas had humbled himself, he might have experienced a sense of the mercy of God. But he hardened his heart against love, and it destroyed him.

Yes, denial and betrayal happen routinely and regularly in our lives. Most of us have experienced denial or betrayal in some way. Most of us have also denied or betrayed others in some way. Denial is so often based in our fear, fear of the consequences of our mistakes. Betrayal happens in our relationships and friendships—perceived or real, small or large—and is always a cause of pain. What happened that holy night in an upper room around a table with Jesus is a continued and continuing experience for each of us, every day.

## PREPARING YOUR UPPER ROOM

These personalities, and how they behaved that night, are all in the context of the most important meal that has ever taken place in history—a meal we are invited to attend in the upper rooms of our lives. It is a transformative meal where the love of the Risen Jesus, despite our shortcomings, continues to empower, change, and guide us.

In the personalities of the apostles Peter and Judas, each of us can see glimmers of our individual life histories. The initial arguments among the apostles at table and the special love shown by John provide a rich context for that night and meal, and guideposts for each of us in the upper rooms in our day.

There has always been a diverse group of personalities at table with the Lord. At this time in history, you and I now are present. We, like the apostles, are unreliable and weak and afraid. We are inconstant in our devotion to our Lord. We deny him, we betray him.

But Jesus is I Am. He is constant.

The One who sits with arms outstretched in the Da Vinci depiction, who sat in the center of the table in that Upper Room, sits now in the center of our hearts with arms outstretched. He died on the cross out of love for us. He is continually with us, welcoming us, and looking at us with his loving, tender gaze, just as he looked at Peter. What he did at table, he continues to do with all our varied and challenged humanity, a variety of personalities that is forever and continually represented in every church, in every upper room, throughout our entire world, where "two or three are gathered together in his name" (Matthew 18:20).

CHAPTER FOUR

# Jesus Washes his Disciples' Feet

As Jesus and his disciples gathered for what turned out to be their
Last Supper before his crucifixion, Jesus performed an utterly
shocking gesture.[10]

—Chris Lowney

## Intentional Service

The washing of feet was one of the most memorable actions that
took place during the Last Supper. It took place in the Upper
Room and gave additional meaning to what transpired there. As Pope
Francis would say in his visit to that Upper Room on May 26, 2014:

> The Upper Room speaks to us of service, of Jesus giving the disciples
> an example by washing their feet. Washing one another's feet signi-
> fies welcoming, accepting, loving and serving one another. It means
> serving the poor, the sick and the outcast.[11]

Throughout the ages, many artists have depicted Jesus washing the feet
of his apostles, and for centuries theologians have discussed its meaning
and implications. This utterly surprising gesture on the part of Jesus
has, even in our day, been a point of conversation for those of us who
are his followers.

Throughout his ministry, every word Jesus spoke and every action
he performed was done with intentionality. He did not waste time or
parse words. Every step he took resonates throughout time, bringing
meaning and purpose to our lives.

The events of the Upper Room were no different. The words, prayers,
and actions of Jesus are, as even he described them, an example for us
to follow. He said: "I have given you a model to follow, so that as I have

*29*

done for you, you should also do" (John 13:15). The act of washing the feet of his disciples was an intentional demonstration of the loving service with which Christ leads. Jesus would later say: "I am the way and the truth and the life" (John 14:6). Washing feet thus becomes the way of Jesus, evidences the truth of Jesus, and gives life for those of us who see Jesus as a model for our lives. It is an incredible example of the humility of our God.

## GETTING INVOLVED

In his first apostolic exhortation, Pope Francis highlights and gives us his understanding of this action by our Lord. He writes:

> Jesus washed the feet of his disciples. The Lord gets involved and he involves his own, as he kneels to wash their feet. He tells his disciples: "You will be blessed if you do this" (John 13:17). An evangelizing community gets involved by word and deed in people's daily lives; it bridges distances, it is willing to abase itself if necessary, and it embraces human life, touching the suffering flesh of Christ in others. (*EG* 24)

Embedded in Pope Francis's words is the call literally to do what Jesus did. Getting involved—touching the suffering, washing feet, feeding the hungry—is not simply a liturgical ritual which takes place annually on Holy Thursday, the Holy Thursday mandatum, as important as that is to keep the memory of Christ's unique action alive for all times. No, as explained by Pope Francis, it is a call to each of us to a similar kind of action.

In the words of Jesus at the Last Supper, after washing the feet of the disciples, he gave them this evangelical command: "If I, therefore, the master and teacher, have washed your feet, you ought to wash one another's feet. I have given you a model to follow, so that as I have done for you, you should also do" (John 13:14–15). In the process, by way of word and example, he gave his followers a new commandment. He told them: "I give you a new commandment: love one another. As I have loved you, so you also should love one another. This is how all will know that you are my disciples, if you have love for one another" (John 13:34–35). Or as St. Paul said in his Letter to the Ephesians: "So be imitators of God, as beloved children, and live in love, as Christ loved us and handed himself over for us as a sacrificial offering to God for a fragrant aroma" (Ephesians 5:1–2).

## Becoming a Servant

John's Gospel is the only Gospel text to include the washing of feet. This is significant. Unlike Mathew, Mark, and Luke, however, John's Gospel does not include the institution of the Eucharist—"Do this in memory of me."

In his book on Jesus of Nazareth, Gerhard Lohfink writes: "Hence the washing of feet before the last meal, which the evangelist John regards as so crucial that he tells of it instead of the universally familiar words of institution" (John 13:1–20).[12]

In a certain way, then, the feet washing in John's Gospel stands in the place of the institution of the Eucharist and helps demonstrate its deeper meaning. What Jesus was instituting in the Upper Room, on the night before he died, was not simply a meal but a significant step closer to the culmination of his salvific mission on the cross, his mission of love for our salvation. And it is precisely his self-gift on the cross at Calvary, that ultimate sign of his salvific love for us, that is symbolically demonstrated in the washing of the feet in the Upper Room. And he commanded his disciples to do the same thing.

By his death and resurrection, each of the disciples of the Lord—and each of us, in ways appropriate to our own vocation—is empowered forever to follow him in the breaking of the bread and the breaking of our bodies out of love for each other. "Do this in memory of me" means, at its deepest level, to exhibit the same humbling abasement, as a servant, that Jesus demonstrated as he knelt to wash the feet of his apostles.

There were several layers of meaning in the act of washing feet, as James Martin points out in his book *Jesus*: "At the time, foot washing was seen as a mark of hospitality, but also a menial task often performed by slaves to welcome a dignitary hosted by the slave's master."[13] According to the Talmud, that authoritative body of Jewish tradition, the washing of feet was forbidden to any Jew except those in slavery. Consider that for a moment. Jesus knew exactly what it meant to wash the feet of his disciples. He knew exactly what was ahead of him that night and in the following days. Knowing all of this, Jesus, "…poured water into a basin and began to wash the disciples' feet and dry them with the towel around his waist" (John 13:5).

Jesus was acting like a humble slave in the Upper Room at a meal he convoked. In that great hymn found in the Letter to the Philippians, St. Paul adopts that image of Jesus who "emptied himself, taking the form of a slave, coming in human likeness; and found human in appearance, he humbled himself, becoming obedient to death, even death on a cross" (Philippians 2:7–8).

In Matthew's Gospel, Jesus's slave-like action was foreshadowed in his response to the mother of Zebedee's sons, who sought preferential seating next to Jesus "in your Kingdom" (Matthew 20:21). Replying that this request was for his Father to determine, Jesus asked them whether they could drink of the chalice he was to drink, the suffering chalice, the cup to be given at the Last Supper. They said they could.

At that meal, Jesus would say: "Drink from it, all of you, for this is

*32*

my blood of the covenant, which will be shed on behalf of many for the forgiveness of sins…" (Matthew 26:27–28). When Jesus asked the sons of Zebedee if they could drink from his chalice, he was asking them whether they could act as slaves—in other words, become like those not with preferred seating at table, but in a role of service to those at the table instead of them. "Rather, whoever wishes to be great among you shall be your servant; whoever wishes to be the first among you shall be your slave" (Matthew 20:26–27).

### Allowing Jesus to Wash Your Feet

The apostles James and John, the sons of Zebedee, wanted to be like Jesus and sought to drink from his chalice of suffering. But when Jesus knelt to wash the feet of Simon Peter, it was too much for the fisherman to accept: "Peter said to him, 'You will never wash my feet.' Jesus answered him, 'Unless I wash you, you will have no inheritance with me'" (John 13:8). Jesus is not meant to be a model in *theory*, he came to live out the active model of God's love for us. Pope Francis writes: "Peter did not want Jesus to wash his feet, but he came to realize that Jesus does not wish to be just an example of how we should wash one another's feet. Only those who have first allowed Jesus to wash their own feet can then offer this service to others."[14]

Jesus explained his actions more fully after he had washed the feet of all of them: "If I, therefore, the master and teacher, have washed your feet, you ought to wash one another's feet. I have given you a model to follow, so that as I have done for you, you should also do. Amen, amen, I say to you, no slave is greater than his master…. If you understand this, blessed are you if you do it" (John 13:14–17).

In the washing of the feet, this supreme example of humble love and service, Jesus teaches us by his example in the Upper Room, hours before his death, the value of being a slave out of love for each other.

He "emptied himself, taking the form of a slave" and demonstrated concretely that washing feet, an example of loving hospitality reserved to slaves, was a radically new way for the Son of Man to serve with love and abasement. And he commanded them, and us, to do the same thing. Such action is at the heart of our faith. Jesus even called it a new commandment, a commandment of loving and humble service. Each one of us should obey the Lord's new commandment to love one another with an abundance of love and humility. It is our identity card as Christians.

In the words of St. John Paul II in his letter to priests:

> Even more than an example of humility offered for our imitation, this action of Jesus, so disconcerting to Peter, is a revelation of the radicalness of God's condescension towards us. In Christ, God has "stripped himself" and has taken on the "form of a slave" even to the utter abasement of the Cross, so that humanity might have access to the depths of God's very life.[15]

This action, precisely at the time that Jesus knew his hour had come, implies that he was committed to the redemptive sacrifice. The washing of feet is linked to the mystery of the Eucharist that they were about to celebrate in the Upper Room. The One who served by washing feet would soon thereafter give himself as food and drink and tell us to do this in his memory. This humble service is tied to and gives meaning to his actions at the table, and his later loving action on the cross. It is how we also live our participation in the Mass—humble, servant-like service. In the words of Father Galot, in his book *The Eucharistic Heart*:

> From then on, the Eucharist has contained within itself the power of humble love that led to the washing of the feet. The command to wash one another's feet (which Jesus gave them) would be stamped on the behavior of the disciples if they sought, in the eucharistic

meal, the humility which would enable them to put themselves in the last place instead of claiming the first, and to serve to the end. Those who receive the body of the Lord and who open themselves to its spiritual influence, are transformed by it in such a way that they adopt the attitude of service and humble devotedness that inspired the institution of the Eucharist.[16]

## PREPARING YOUR UPPER ROOM

Our challenge daily, in the upper rooms of our lives where we eat and have fellowship with those closest to us, is to seek out concrete and specific opportunities to give of ourselves to others in need of love and respect. And so many such opportunities exist if we are sensitive and on the lookout for them. Such loving service defines being a Christian ever anew.

Our world is replete with the suffering flesh of Christ awaiting us, as his followers, and awaiting our embrace as that suffering presents itself to us. The washing of dirty feet, a lasting memory and command of the Upper Room, is in effect a paradigm for the many, many acts of Christian humble service that have become a way of life for those who seek to follow Jesus faithfully and continually. It is our challenge and joy.

There is a beautiful hymn entitled: *"Ubi caritas et amor, Deus ibi est."* ("Where charity and love are, God is there.") Holy Communion is the feast of love, salvific love, the love of humble service. As we are transformed more and more in communion with Jesus in the Eucharist, we take on his love in our actions. Where charity and love are, there is he. The Eucharist makes him visible and possible in our lives. It is how we live the Mass and model every day this example of Jesus in the Upper Room.

CHAPTER FIVE

# Foot Washing as an Icon of Catholic Social Teaching

The Lord appeared to Abraham by the oak of Mamre, as he sat in the entrance of his tent, while the day was growing hot. Looking up, he saw three men standing near him. When he saw them, he ran from the entrance of the tent to greet them; and bowing to the ground, he said: "Sir, if it please you, do not go on past your servant. Let some water be brought, that you may bathe your feet, and then rest under the tree."

—Genesis 18:1–4

## Mercy Is the Face of God

For Jesus, the washing of feet was an act of humble service, just as it was for Abraham as he hurried to extend hospitality to the Lord under the oaks of Mamre. And yet, by taking up the basin and towel and ministering to his disciples, the Lord infused this act of humility with love, the kind of love that transforms all those who bear witness to it.

There are so many ways to sow love with the same practicality as did the Lord in that Upper Room, taking up the basin and performing the task normally reserved for the lowest-ranking servant. In doing this, the Lord showed his followers that the grace of humility must accompany our acts of charity. Whether feeding the hungry, giving drink to the thirsty, clothing the naked, visiting the imprisoned, sheltering the homeless, visiting the sick and burying the dead—the grace of humility makes these corporal works of mercy and charity particularly beautiful, particularly grace-giving. They are concrete ways in which we are sensitive and attentive to the concrete needs of others.

In addition, the spiritual works of mercy, works with focus on the souls and spiritual lives of others, are also profound acts of charity. They include admonishing the sinner, instructing the ignorant, counseling the doubtful, comforting the sorrowful, bearing wrongs patiently, forgiving all injuries, and praying for the living and the dead. Properly understood, then, mercy is the face of God's love as it makes contact with another and triggers conversion of heart by virtue of concrete acts both spiritual and corporal.

In fact, loving service is an essential trait of our Christian identity. In his morning meditation on April 30, 2015, Pope Francis said, "Christian identity is service and service is a way of life," pointing to the example of Christ himself:

> Jesus washes the feet of the Apostles. After washing their feet, he says to them: "Truly, truly, I say to you, a servant is not greater than his master; nor is he who is sent greater than he who sent him. If you know these things, blessed are you if you do them. Do unto others as I have done unto you. As I have come to you as a servant, you must be servants of one another, serve."[17]

I am constantly amazed at the incredible generosity of so many followers of Jesus. There is such a direct link to the frequent feasting on the body and blood of Jesus at Mass—not only Sunday but daily Mass—and the work of Christian service. It is as if the living body and blood of Jesus overcomes each person and makes his hands and feet and heart their own—a eucharistic heart. I think of so many who donate time in pro-bono activities of all types from legal and medical work to those who clean the bed pans of people too sick to help themselves, and those who donate time in our parishes and other institutions of service. These are concrete ways of "washing feet" and of living the Eucharistic love that transforms us at Mass. They are integral to our spirituality.

And at its core, the washing of feet is an icon for what has developed as Catholic social teaching (*USCCA* 421–424). This teaching has often been considered the Church's best kept secret. And at the heart of Catholic social teaching is the dignity of the human person. In every age, the human person, and the dignity of the human person is challenged in different ways, but that dignity should be seen through the prism of the washing of feet. Concern for and love of the human person is central to our faith. Each of us is made, after all, in the image and likeness of God and redeemed by his Son, Jesus Christ.

## THE DIGNITY OF THE HUMAN PERSON

At the outset, it is important to underscore that all other principles of Catholic social teaching build from this foundational principle of the life and dignity of the human person. It is in the continued loving care of every human person, especially the most vulnerable, that we highlight their dignity and worth. When we wash the feet of one person in need, we wash the feet of every person who is suffering and vulnerable.

Consistent Church teaching underscores this important point. For example, in his Apostolic Exhortation *The Joy of the Gospel*, Pope Francis states:

> The dignity of each human person and the pursuit of the common good are concerns which ought to shape all economic policies. At times, however, they seem to be a mere addendum imported from without in order to fill out a political discourse lacking in perspectives or plans for true and integral development. How many words prove irksome to this system.[18]

Dignity is given to all humanity by God. It is because God created and loves us that we have value. Throughout history, papal teaching has reflected this remarkable truth. For example, St. John Paul II, in the encyclical letter *Centesimus Annus,* promulgated on May 1, 1991, to coincide with the 100th anniversary of the publication of Pope Leo XIII's great social encyclical *Rerum Novarum*, writes:

> From this point forward it will be necessary to keep in mind that the main thread and, in a certain sense, the guiding principle of Pope Leo's Encyclical, and of all of the Church's social doctrine, is a *correct view of the human person* and of his unique value, inasmuch as "man...is the only creature on earth which God willed for itself" (*RN* 38). God has imprinted his own image and likeness on man (cf. Genesis 1:26), conferring upon him an incomparable dignity, as the Encyclical frequently insists.[19]

Humanity is unique in all of creation. God sees each sparrow that falls to the ground (Matthew 10:29). He robes the flowers in splendor (Luke 12:27). Yet how much more does he love you? He counts the hairs on your head and knits you together in your mother's womb (Matthew 10:30, Psalm 139:13). It was for *you* that God sent his only Son. Every single human is loved with this intimate, unfathomable, selfless love of God. This reality is what bestows dignity to each of us, and it is vital that we cherish the dignity of each person in response.

In *Mater et Magistra,* St. John XXIII writes, "The permanent validity of the Catholic Church's social teaching admits of no doubt."[20] He continues, "This teaching rests on one basic principle: individual human beings are the foundation, the cause and the end of every social institution."[21] St. John XXIII concludes by stating that "On this basic principle, which guarantees the sacred dignity of the individual, the Church constructs her social teaching."[22]

## THE SOURCE OF OUR DIGNITY

It is important to assert that it is Christ himself, "the image of the invisible God" who reveals man to himself, who fully discloses what it is to be human and manifests the nobility of our vocation. Our human dignity is thus inexorably linked to the very person of Jesus Christ, "the way, the truth and the life." So what does Jesus reveal about the human condition, our human dignity—you and me?

He reveals that we have a divine destiny and that our human condition, a condition he took on himself, has a "new" dignity that is worthy of protecting and safeguarding from conception until natural death. And Jesus gives us a clear example, by his life, that only in one's loving self-giving does the meaning of one's life become clear. Christ showed that to us most clearly by his death on the cross, all out of love for us, his divine generosity.

Our God became man to come close to us—to pitch his tent amongst us—and to do so precisely where we are, in our human condition. In so doing, he revealed the meaning of our human condition. The Creator of the Universe incarnated himself, uniting himself indissolubly with human nature, to the point of really being, in the words of the Nicene Creed, "God from God, light from light" and at the same time, man, true man. And by his Incarnation: "He, the Son of God, has in a certain way united himself" with each one of us, without exception. "He worked with human hands, he thought with a human mind. He acted with a human will, and with a human heart, he loved."[23]

By embracing our human condition—in everything but sin—Jesus revealed the new dignity and the surpassing worth of our human condition and the need in love to care for the human person. He tied and linked himself to us forever—to each one of us—by taking on our human flesh. He ennobled the human condition and raised it to the level of his divinity.

This is the theological basis of our daily challenge to protect and advance human life from conception until natural death, to promote the dignity of the human person at every stage of development, and to seek the peaceful resolution of national and international conflicts. Through his humble service, from the moment he was born in that stable in Bethlehem to the moment he laid down his own life out of love for us, Jesus gives ultimate meaning to the human condition in all its brokenness by raising our human condition to the level of the divine in the victories of the human spirit.

To a certain extent, then, each one of us was born in Bethlehem. We share, by his birth, a newness of life, the beginning of our share in a new life that will last forever. It is for that reason that the Church continues strongly to protect all human life and encourage the "washing of feet" as a lasting model of that protection. Each human life—born and unborn—is stamped with the face of God and receives our new dignity in Christ. In other words, "'The social order and its development must invariably work to the benefit of the human person, since the order of things is to be subordinate to the order of persons, and not the other way around.' Respect for human dignity can in no way be separated from obedience to this principle" (*CSD* 132, GS 26).

Our newfound dignity is made possible by our Baptism into Christ Jesus. It is a life "worthy of the Gospel of Christ" (Philippians 1:27). Christians are called to be imitators of Christ and especially of his loving care for those in need, those whose very dignity became challenged.

## Preparing Your Upper Room

Jesus has given us a "model" of service that is so unique. Washing feet is symbolic of all that Jesus was and continues to be for us. It is a unique way to be like Jesus, the Jesus of the Upper Room, and the Jesus who continues to be everywhere we are. Washing of feet is an unforgettable dimension of the very life of Jesus and should be an integral part of our lives. It is a quintessential Upper Room experience awaiting daily imitation in our lives as followers of Jesus as we seek to ennoble and protect the human dignity that is vested in every human person—that first and fundamental principle of Catholic social teaching.

# CHAPTER SIX

# LAST SUPPER DISCOURSES OF LOVE AND THE PRAYER OF JESUS

The Eucharist is the gift that Jesus Christ makes of himself, thus revealing to us God's infinite love for every man and woman. This wondrous sacrament makes manifest that "greater" love which led him to "lay down his life for his friends" (John 15:13). Jesus did indeed love them "to the end" (John 13:1).... What amazement must the Apostles have felt in witnessing what the Lord did and said during that Supper! It was unlike any dinner, I am sure, that they had ever experienced or any of us will ever experience. What wonder must the eucharistic mystery also awaken in our own hearts!

—Pope Benedict XVI, *Sacramentum Caritas,* 1

## THROUGH HIS WORDS

In addition to the institution of the priesthood, through which the apostolic mission of Christ entrusted to his apostles would continue, the Lord also instituted in that same room the sacrament of love. It is the sacrament of the Eucharist where he feeds them and each of us on his very body and blood out of love. It is a mystery of unfailing and unconditional love, a mystery revealed in words and deeds.

After he washed the feet of his disciples, he began to speak to them at great length. In this chapter, our focus will be on the words of Jesus. These passages are akin to a series of farewell discourses and prayer, recorded only in the Gospel of John in four chapters—John 14—17.

It seems, from the tone of his words, as if Jesus was having a hard time saying farewell to those closest to him in those final hours before his suffering, death and resurrection. He spoke from his heart and out of love. These Upper Room talks were tender, loving and reassuring. It was as if he were getting his affairs in order. Jesus would not leave them orphans. He encouraged them to "Remain in me, as I remain in you" (John 15:4).

As he communicated his love for them by the washing their feet, these farewell discourses represent the love of Jesus communicated to them through words—words designed to console and encourage. It makes sense that Jesus would both act and speak at the Last Supper because our God has always revealed himself and communicated his love to us in words and deeds. The Second Vatican Council insisted, after all, that "the economy of Revelation is realized by deeds and words, which are intrinsically bound up with each other" (*DV* 2). In each of the sacraments, for example, the special means by which Jesus continues his ministry in our day, we experience that grace-filled ministry of Jesus through words and deeds.

So the apostles watched Jesus wash their feet and now they were challenged to listen to his words. Watching and listening—combined ways of being drawn into the richness of what was happening in the Upper Room on the night before our Savior died!

## WORDS OF COMFORT

It must have been difficult for the apostles to understand the true meaning of his message to them that night. Here was their friend and teacher delivering what was apparently a leave-taking message as they sat at the table in celebration of the Passover. The tone of that night must have varied widely from moment to moment—from joyful celebration to tender service to heart-wrenching words of farewell. Yet, they listened to the words of his heart addressed to them, his closest friends.

In John 14, Jesus encouraged his apostles twice not to be afraid or let their hearts be troubled. He had to leave them to go to the Father to prepare a place for them but he would come back again: "I will come back and take you to myself, so that where I am you also may be" (John 14:3). He defined himself in that well-known line from Scripture: "I am the way and the truth and the life" (John 14:6). It is only through him, the "way," that access to the Father is made possible. As he told Philip, "Whoever has seen me has seen the Father" (John 14:9).

He was on his way to the Father, and his words that night lay the foundation for the sending of the Holy Spirit: "And I will ask the Father, and he will give you another Advocate to be with you always, the Spirit of truth . ." (John 14:16–17). At the same time, he assured them that he would not leave them as orphans when he left them: "In a little while the world will no longer see me, but you will see me, because I live and you will live. On that day you will realize that I am in my Father and you are in me and I in you" (John 14:19–20).

Though Jesus was leaving—and though it grieved him to do so—he was offering his dearest friends incredible comfort. He assures them that they will not be alone, no matter what. He promises them that there is a purpose in his departure—he is going to make a place for them. Consider how those words must have sounded to the men around that table! Jesus was going to prepare a place for them in heaven. Their God was doing everything in his power for the salvation of his children—even submitting to death on the cross. In effect, he tells them that they should rejoice that he is leaving them to go to the Father who is greater than he: "And now I have told you this before it happens, so that when it happens you may believe" (John 14:29).

Jesus does not stop at the reassurance that his followers will never be alone. He also gives them the incredible gift of his peace. Before departing, Jesus tells them: "Peace I leave with you, my peace I give to you" (John 14:27). As if to enshrine these specific words of peace from

Jesus on the night before he died, these words from St. John's Gospel, the Church gives us a prayer during Mass. It can be found as a part of the rite of peace at Mass:

> Lord Jesus Christ, who said to your Apostles: Peace I leave you, my peace I give you, look not on our sins, but on the faith of your Church, and graciously grant her peace and unity in accordance with your will.

These words, revealed words from the Upper Room, are spoken at every Mass, every time we gather for Eucharist.

### WORDS OF WARNING AND INSTRUCTION

As we move onto John 15, Jesus defines himself as the "true" vine. He says, "I am the true vine, and my Father is the vine grower. He takes away every branch in me that does not bear fruit, and every one that does he prunes so that it bears more fruit" (John 15:1–2). He underscores, over and over again, the need for his apostles to remain in him: "Remain in me, as I remain in you. Just as a branch cannot bear fruit on its own unless it remains on the vine, so neither can you unless you remain in me" (John 14:4). To underscore this point, Jesus uses the word *remain* twelve times in John 14—once for each apostle.

This has Eucharistic overtones: "Whoever eats my flesh and drinks my blood remains in me and I in him" (John 6:56). How appropriate for the Upper Room where Jesus instituted the Eucharist! Jesus so wants his apostles not to forget him and for us not to forget him that he speaks the words over and over. It is as if he is tapping out an unforgettable rhythm on the door of our hearts with the repetition of his message in the Upper Room. As he says in Revelation 3:20, "Behold, I stand at the door and knock. If anyone hears my voice and opens the door, then I will enter his house and dine with him, and he with me." That night, with his continuing instruction for the apostles to remain in him, Jesus was standing at the door of their hearts (and ours), knocking.

The Christian life consists in remaining in Jesus. As Pope Francis has said: "To remain in Jesus means to be united to him, to receive life from him, to receive love from him, to receive the Holy Spirit from him."[24]

Along with the message to remain in him, he reiterates that he chose them and appointed them "to go and bear fruit that will remain" (John 14:16). Jesus even talks about persecution—foreshadowing the persecution the apostles and those who follow him will face.

Tradition has it that all but two of the apostles died a martyr's death. The Book of Acts details many of the trials these men faced in their own ministries, including imprisonment, stoning, and crucifixion. The zealotry with which the early Christians were persecuted was enormous. Even Saul, before his experience on the road to Damascus, dedicated his life to stopping the spread of Jesus's message. Such persecution continues in our day—recently and most graphically in the Middle East, Africa and parts of Asia.

The Lord's specific challenge to them, moreover, was to bear fruit. That was their mission and our mission. We are to bear the fruit that comes from linkage to him. At the Last Supper, he is laying the foundation hours before his own suffering and death, challenging his apostles, and those who would follow him, to be productive by remaining in his love. You and I have that challenge every day.

In John 16, he is coming to the end of his beautiful and heartfelt words of encouragement: "A little while and you will no longer see me, and again a little while later and you will see me" (John 16:16). It is hard to believe that he was saying this to them knowing full well that within hours he would be brutally beaten in preparation for his crucifixion. But he was concerned for his friends and sought to prepare them, for grief had entered their hearts. He speaks words of warning, words of instruction, yes, but mostly, he speaks words of comfort: "But I tell you the truth, it is better for you that I go. For if I do not go, the Advocate will not come to you. But if I go, I will send him to you" (John 16:7).

As with any emotional conversation, sometimes the recipients can only handle so much. This was true of the disciples, too, and Jesus understood their limits. He says, "I have much more to tell you, but you cannot bear it now. But when he comes, the Spirit of truth, he will guide you to all truth" (John 16:12–13) and "your grief will become joy" (John 16:20).

At the end, after this long address, the apostles made a profession of faith. It seemed as though they were moved at last to understand, at least in part, who Jesus was. After Jesus told them once again that he had come from the Father and was now returning to him, they declared: "Now you are talking plainly, and not in any figure of speech. Now we realize that you know everything and that you do not need to have anyone question you. Because of this we believe that you came from God" (John 16:29–30). And he reassured them one more time: "In the world you will have trouble, but take courage, I have conquered the world" (John 16:33).

## WORDS OF PRAYER

Finally, we focus on chapter seventeen of St. John's Gospel, when "his hour" had finally come. This chapter has been referred to in the Christian Tradition as "the 'priestly' prayer of Jesus," the longest prayer offered in any of the four Gospels (CCC 2747). It is as if Jesus is allowing us to eavesdrop on his threefold prayer to the Father—a prayer for himself, for his disciples, and for those, including ourselves, who would follow him. These words were designed to reassure his apostles that he was and would continue to intercede for them prayerfully, even after he left them for the last time.

Not only did Jesus teach his apostles to pray the Our Father during his public ministry, but now, in the Upper Room, he teaches his apostles, and us, to pray by his personal example and specific words. This took place minutes before he would leave the Upper Room for the Garden of Gethsemane to be arrested. It was the climax of the last discourses of Jesus.

Jesus's "priestly" prayer begins simply: "Father, the hour has come" (John 17:l). It is the long-awaited "Hour" toward which his entire mission on earth had been directed. It is the hour, in the words of Pope Benedict XVI, where Jesus's heart was pierced and "from whose pierced heart flows the love of God" (DCE 7).

In that Upper Room, Jesus would first pray for himself as he faced his impending destiny on the cross. He prays, "Now glorify me, Father, with you, with the glory that I had with you before the world began" (John 17:5). He allows his apostles to hear what is in his prayerful heart as he prepares to die. He reminds the Father that he glorified him "on earth by accomplishing the work that [he] gave [him] to do" (John 17:4). In effect, Jesus now prays to ask the Father to crown that work that Jesus undertook during his earthly ministry.

Next, Jesus prays for his disciples: "I pray for them. I do not pray for the world but for the ones you have given me, because they are yours…" (John 17:9). It is a prayer of protection because he will no longer be with them. The disciples, who were listening to every word he spoke, heard this prayer and must have taken consolation from it. Jesus continues, "I do not ask that you take them out of the world but that you keep them from the evil one" (John 17:15). He prays that they be consecrated in truth, proclaiming, "Your word is truth" (John 17:17). As Pope Francis explains: "But Jesus, at the Last Supper, in the prayer to the Father, what did he pray? 'But please, Father, keep these disciples from falling into the world, from falling into worldliness.' Worldliness is a subtle sin—it is more than a sin—it is a sinful state of soul."[25]

Finally, Jesus prays for all believers in the future (John 17: 20–23). It is worth pondering that, very soon before his agony and death, Jesus was praying to the Father for you and me. We were on his mind and in his prayerful heart just as much as those who were physically present with him in the Upper Room. He says, "I pray not only for them (his disciples), but also for those who will believe in me through their word…" (John 17:20). Yes, Jesus is praying for future generations of believers on the night before he died. What a remarkable thought! He continues to intercede for us from heaven every day and every moment.

As Pope Francis reminds us in one of his weekday homilies: "… and so it is that every day, Jesus intercedes. When we, for one thing or the other, are feeling a little down, let us remember that it is he who prays for us, intercedes for us continually. So many times we forget this: 'Jesus…but yes, it's finished, he's gone to heaven, sent us the Holy Spirit, the story's over.' No! Even now, in every moment, Jesus intercedes."[26] How comforting this is for you and me! We have an intercessor in heaven who continually intercedes for us.

### Preparing Your Upper Room

After his prayer in the Upper Room, Jesus proceeds directly to the Garden of Gethsemane where he will be betrayed and suffer and die for our salvation. But he leaves the Upper Room with prayer on his lips and a heart full of love.

Considering this, it is impossible not to think of the Upper Room as a room of prayer, a room where Jesus demonstrates to his apostles the importance of intercessory and personal prayer in our daily lives. The Upper Room is coterminous with the word prayer—an "art" and "gift" which is absolutely essential to the Christian life. As Pope Francis writes: "If we don't pray, we might be good pastoral and spiritual entre-preneurs, but without prayer the Church becomes an NGO, she does not have the *unctio Spiritus Sancti*. Prayer is the first step, because it is opening oneself to the Lord to be able to open oneself to others."[27]

Words of love and words of prayerful support for his friends, his apos-tles, were an integral part of Jesus's prayer and witness in the Upper Room. The Eucharist is the highest form of prayer. It was instituted in the Upper Room. In addition, Jesus models intercessory prayer in that same room—prayer for him, his apostles, and for each of us. How then can we not embrace more deeply the exhortation, as his followers, to pray constantly? The prayerful example of Christ is assuredly a lasting and defining gift to us, an Upper Room gift full of love, the unsurpassed love of our God.

CHAPTER SEVEN

# TERM OF ENDEARMENT: JESUS CALLS APOSTLES "FRIENDS"

If Jesus wishes to be our friend—and he has told us that he does—then, at least by analogy, it would behoove us to reflect on the model human friendship we have had or continue to have. It might give us some insight into friendship with God and how that friendship, for sure a developing relationship, could be defined and experienced.

## THE GREATEST COMMANDMENT

The topic of friendship is a theme very often written about, a theme produced on Broadway, and even used in refrains of songs. It means different things to different people. In the Upper Room, Jesus specifically and somewhat unexpectedly talks about friendship as well. He sets a fairly high bar for friendship, however, when he tells his apostles: "No one has greater love than this, to lay down one's life for one's friends" (John 15:13). These words foreshadow what he was about to undergo in his suffering and death on the cross, all out of love.

When Jesus set the bar for friendship—saying that there is no greater love than sacrificial love—he knew that the standard he was setting was one only he, our God, could achieve. Humans are, of course, capable of loving sacrificially. This love is seen every day. Parents sacrificially love their children. Spouses show loving sacrifice to one another. Even friends regularly sacrifice time, energy, money, and many other things for each other.

But it is incredibly rare to see the standard Jesus described in today's world. So rare, in fact, that when it does happen, we tend to label it "heroism." There are those who sacrifice their lives for their family,

55

friends, country, and religion. Only Jesus sacrificed himself for *everyone*, even those who took part in his betrayal, torture, and murder. His sacrifice is available to each of us, and he did it knowing that we would reject him time and again. Still, he did not hesitate. He defined sacrificial love with his words to the apostles, and then again through his actions on the cross.

Jesus set the ultimate standard of sacrificial love, and he also gave very clear and precise instructions to us. He says to his apostles, and to us, "You are my friends if you do what I command you'" (John 15:14). What a tremendous offer—to be his friend, friends of God! And he tells them as well that he no longer calls them slaves because a slave does not know what his master is doing: "I have called you friends, because I have told you everything I have heard from my Father" (John 15:15).

Jesus must have endeared himself to his apostles by calling them his "friends" (John 15:14). And yet, he was speaking to you and me as well. What a beautiful offer, to be a friend of Jesus if we do what he commands. He has made his command very clear: "You shall love the Lord, your God, with all your heart, with all your soul, and with all your mind. This is the greatest and the first commandment. The second is like it: You shall love your neighbor as yourself" (Matthew 22:37–38).

### Living in Love

Love is one of the most frequently misused words in our culture. There are many declarations of love in our world today, and not all of them are godly. The radio is bursting with songs about love, from old crooners reminding us that love as "a many-splendored thing," to teen pop stars wailing about love at first sight. But if our friendship with God depends on what he commands of us—and love is the greatest command—it might be helpful to reflect on Jesus's type of love, his understanding of the meaning of the word love.

For followers of Jesus, for Christians, the word love represents something very specific and precise. It is not just a word. It represents a reality—the very life of God, our God who took on flesh, lived, suffered, and laid down his life for his friends. The cross, that incredible symbol of love, reminds us of the unique Christian meaning of love.

St. John tells us, "Beloved, let us love one another, because love is of God; everyone who loves is begotten by God and knows God…God is love" (1 John 4:7–8). Love is God. And God is alive. Therefore, the reality of love is a living reality. Love is word and deed; it is not just sentiment, it is action.

We know God when we see a lover, when we see someone who wears the face of God's kind of love. It means giving oneself for someone without condition and often with sacrifice. It is, for example, what parents do day in and day out, what grandparents live. It means how children are taught to interact with their brothers and sisters, and the best teaching is by way of example.

God's love is active and dynamic. It is always caught up in the perpetual motion of creating, protecting, saving, sacrificing, forgiving, warning, punishing, leading, and feeding. And you and I are the objects of this perpetual motion we call love. We are the objects and subjects of God's love.

The Scripture is filled with examples of the love of God revealed in Jesus Christ. It is God who runs after the prodigal son and gives him a welcoming embrace. It is God who leaves the ninety-nine sheep to look for the one lost sheep. It is God—the Good Samaritan—who cared for the half-dead victim on the road and brought him help when a priest and Levite respectively walked away.

God's kind of love is always taking the initiative, as Scripture tells us. "In this is love: not that we have loved God, but that he loved us and sent his Son as expiation for our sins" (1 John 4:10). He has loved us first and continues to demonstrate that kind of love each and every day.

## TRUE FRIENDSHIP

Like love, friendship is a concept that has been watered down and twisted in today's world. We can look at Scripture and see the true definition, of course: "A friend is a friend at all times" (Proverbs 17:17). In other words, a friend never leaves us. A friend *remains*. Remember Jesus's words in the last chapter? "Remain in me, as I remain in you" (John 15:4). Jesus promised to remain with us in the Upper Room, and his promise endures. He also clearly stated what friendship with him entails: "You are my friends if you do what I command you" (John 15:14).

If Jesus wishes to be our friend, and he has told us that he does, then, at least by analogy, it would behoove us to reflect on our human friendships. It might give us some insight into friendship with God and how that friendship, an ever-developing relationship, might be defined. At its basis, it is about true sacrificial love for each other after the example of Jesus.

A genuine friendship requires keeping in touch with each other. It requires, and this is often tested, being present in times of need as well as times of joy. It means truly caring for another. Friendship means building each other up rather than tearing each other down. True friends remain, or as Proverbs tells us, a true friend is a friend *at all times*. It is not easy. The best of friends are there to help and encourage when someone is in a challenging predicament.

Concretely, it means visiting hospitals and nursing homes and prisons. It means, for example, accompanying a friend to weekly chemo treatments. Friendship can require sacrifice and love. And this type of sacrificial love is becoming more and more necessary in our day.

Friendship is another word for companionship—a one-on-one relationship between two people marked by mutual honesty, love, and openness without any fear of reprisals. Faithful spouses exemplify that type of relationship. Friendship requires the ability to listen to each other, even when one might not be interested in a particular topic or issue. It is not overly competitive or based on primarily utilitarian interests. True friendship is an encounter with each other wherever one might be. Friendship is tested over time. One has a "feeling" that a certain relationship is truly one of friendship and can and should be developed more and more.

In his encyclical letter *Deus Caritas Est* (God is Love), Pope Benedict writes: "Being Christian is not the result of an ethical choice or a lofty idea, but the encounter with an event, a person, which gives life a new horizon and a decisive direction" (*DCE* 1). He is speaking here about an encounter with Jesus. Not unlike our human friendships, an encounter with the person Jesus is the basis of our friendship with him. Many of the qualities about which we just spoke in terms of human friendships apply, at least by analogy, to an encounter with Jesus.

Above all, we are privileged friends of Jesus when we love each other with the kind of sacrificial love Jesus endured for us. It is a love that he makes possible within us, a love specifically designed to be shared and given away. As if to make his fundamental command perfectly clear, he tells his apostles and each of us: "I give you a new commandment: love one another. As I have loved you, so you also should love one another" (John 13:34). Our friendship with God depends on this. How privileged we are!

## PREPARING YOUR UPPER ROOM

In the thirteenth chapter of St. Paul's first letter to the Corinthian Christians, he expounded on the many qualities of love in a passage that has been the basis of countless wedding homilies. And yet, this passage also reminds us of the quintessential characteristics of all authentic human love, whether within the particular context of marriage, or in other types of human connection. In many cases, putting these characteristics into practice requires true "self-giving" and self-sacrifice, the kind of love Jesus calls each of us to live by.

> If I speak in human and angelic tongues but do not have love, I am a resounding gong or a clashing cymbal. And if I have the gift of prophecy and comprehend all mysteries and all knowledge; if I have all faith so as to move mountains but do not have love, I am nothing....
>
> Love is patient, love is kind. It is not jealous, [love] is not pompous, it is not inflated, it is not rude, it does not seek its own interests, it is not quick-tempered, it does not brood over injury, it does not rejoice over wrongdoing but rejoices with the truth. It bears all things, believes all things, hopes all things, endures all things.
>
> Love never fails.
>
> —1 Corinthians 13:1–8

As we conclude this part of the book, we take a moment to reflect upon this passage in order to meet God in the upper rooms of our hearts, allowing him to shine light on those parts of our lives where the seeds of love lie dormant, waiting to burst forth in new life. This kind of love is essential to understanding and living the love of God made manifest in his Son, Jesus Christ—a model for our love for each other.

# THE UPPER ROOM—
# POST-RESURRECTION APPEARANCES

Michelangelo Merisi da Caravaggio, *The Incredulity of St. Thomas,*
1601-1602. Sanssouci, Potsdam, Germany.

The Upper Room, until this point, has been a place of institution. It was there that Jesus instituted the Eucharist and Holy Orders. He demonstrated God's active love through both word (his discourses and prayer) and deed (washing of feet). The *Catechism of the Catholic Church* teaches that Jesus, "In order to leave them (his apostles) a pledge of (his) love, in order never to depart from his own and to make them sharers in his Passover…instituted the Eucharist as the memorial of his death and Resurrection, and commanded his apostles to celebrate it until his return" (*CCC* 1337).

How appropriate, then, that the Risen Lord would appear in that same Upper Room, where the Eucharist was instituted on the night before his death, on that first Easter Sunday night immediately after his resurrection! For the Eucharist is both a "memorial of his death *and* Resurrection."

It is, after all, the Risen Lord we receive in Holy Communion, his Body and Blood, the pledge of eternal life to come. Or as the priest says at Mass, that which was instituted in that Upper Room: "May this mingling of the Body and Blood of our Lord Jesus Christ bring eternal life to us who receive it." And particularly on the day we celebrate the Resurrection, "at Sunday Mass, Christians relive with particular intensity the experience of the Apostles on the evening of Easter when the Risen Lord appeared to them as they were gathered together" (*DD* 33).

Tradition holds it that the post-resurrection appearances of Jesus took place in the same Upper Room where the Last Supper took place. This was confirmed by Pope Francis during his visit to the Upper Room in 2014 where he stated that the same Upper Room was also the place of the Pentecost.[28]

Part Two of this book focuses on John 20:19–29—the appearances of the Risen Lord in the Upper Room. First, it is the Risen Jesus's appearance to his apostles there on Easter Sunday night after his death and resurrection and second his appearance in the Upper Room a week later (John 20:26).

I highlight, as well, three specific points from John 20:19–29, all of which take place in the Upper Room. They are the coming of the Holy Spirit, the forgiveness of sins, and Thomas's profession of Easter faith a week later. All three are integral to the life of the Church today and our personal spiritual journeys each and every day.

The fundamental challenge, then, in our day, is to experience the same Holy Spirit, the permanent gift of Easter, breathed on the apostles by the Risen One, in the forgiveness of their sins, and like Thomas, the challenge to manifest ever anew our living faith in the Lord Jesus. With great confidence, we embrace and yield to the movement of grace in the upper rooms of our concrete lives.

# CHAPTER EIGHT

# The Coming of the Holy Spirit

In the beginning when God created the heavens and the earth…a wind from God swept over the face of the waters. Then God said, "Let there be light"; and there was light.

—Genesis 1:1–3

In the beginning was the Word, and the Word was with God, and the Word was God…in him was life, and the life was the light of all people.

—John 1:1, 4

## The Advocate

After the crucifixion of Jesus, Scripture tells us that the disciples were in the Upper Room and the doors were locked "for fear of the Jews" (John 20:19). Considering all that had just transpired—the nighttime arrest of Jesus, his trial, the beatings, and violent crucifixion—it is no wonder the disciples were afraid. A man they knew to be innocent had just been slain, and for all they knew, they were next. The atmosphere of the Upper Room was one of tense apprehension, grief, and fear.

It was in that setting that Jesus suddenly appeared in his risen state and twice said to them "Peace be with you" (John 20:19, 21). Imagine their surprise, their relief, their confusion, and their joy at that moment. They could scarcely believe their eyes. The friend and teacher, the same one who had led them in prayer in that room only nights ago, had been crucified. They had no doubt of his death. And suddenly, he was there, among them, reassuring them with his peace. He showed them his hands and his side. And he "breathed on them and said to them, 'receive the holy Spirit. Whose sins you forgive are forgiven them, and whose sins you retain are retained'" (John 20:22–23).

St. John Paul II writes, regarding that text: "All the details of this key-text of John's Gospel have their own eloquence, especially if we read them in reference to the words spoken in the same Upper Room at the beginning of the Paschal events."[29] He had to be referring to Jesus's prediction of his sending the Advocate. I am sure they had no idea what Jesus meant when he said, "When the Advocate comes whom I will send you from the Father, the Spirit of truth that proceeds from the Father, he will testify to me" (John 15:26).

This is our first introduction to the Holy Spirit, or the Advocate. Jesus breathes on them and through his breath—further proof that he is the Risen Lord—they receive the Holy Spirit. "With those words of Jesus the Holy Spirit is revealed and at the same time made present as the Love that works in the depths of the Paschal Mystery, as the source of the salvific power of the Cross of Christ, and as the gift of new and eternal life."[30]

## PENTECOST

There are two accounts of Pentecost and the descent of the Holy Spirit. John 20, the text we are reflecting upon in this chapter, is often referred to as the Johannine Pentecost. In John's Gospel, the Holy Spirit comes on Easter Sunday night. By depicting the coming of the Holy Spirit so close to his death and resurrection, John emphasizes that the dying, rising, and sending of the Holy Spirit are actually seen as one single mystery, all part of one whole. It is one Paschal (or Easter) Mystery.

By contrast, in the second account of Pentecost found in Acts 1:1–13, Luke describes the coming of the Holy Spirit fifty days after Easter—hence *Pentecost*, a word which derives from the Greek word meaning fifty.

In *Evangelii Gaudium,* Pope Francis is clear about the role of the Holy Spirit, a role displayed in the Upper Room on that first Easter night. He writes:

> Yet there is no greater freedom than that of allowing oneself to be guided by the Holy Spirit, renouncing the attempt to plan and control everything to the last detail, and instead letting him enlighten, guide and direct us, leading us wherever he wills. The Holy Spirit knows well what is needed in every time and place. This is what it means to be mysteriously fruitful![31]

The Holy Spirit, the permanent gift of Easter, is another lasting gift of that Upper Room!

### RECEIVING THE HOLY SPIRIT IN YOUR UPPER ROOM

In the Catechism we read, "By his Death and his Resurrection, Jesus is constituted in glory as Lord and Christ (cf. Acts 2:36). From his fullness, he poured out the Holy Spirit on the apostles and the Church" (*CCC* 746). And a little later in the text, "The Holy Spirit, whom Christ the head pours out on his members, builds, animates, and sanctifies the Church. She is the sacrament of the Holy Trinity's communion with men" (*CCC* 747).

Consider for a moment what it must have been like when the Lord first appeared to the apostles after the Resurrection in that Upper Room. They were not expecting to see Jesus when he appeared and breathed on them. How do we experience the unexpected presence of Christ in our own lives? How do we respond to "brushes" with the Holy Spirit?

Recall the experience of your own confirmation, when the gifts of the Holy Spirit you received at baptism were strengthened and enriched with a fresh anointing of the Holy Spirit. How have you experienced those gifts in your life since that time? For sure, you want those gifts to be renewed in your life! And so we pray for the coming of the Holy Spirit in our lives:

Come, Holy Spirit, fill the hearts of your faithful and kindle in them the fire of your love. Send forth your Spirit and they shall be created. And you shall renew the face of the earth.

O God, who by the light of the Holy Spirit, did instruct the hearts of the faithful, grant that by the same Holy Spirit we may be truly wise and ever enjoy his consolations, through Christ Our Lord, Amen.

# CHAPTER NINE

# JESUS FORGIVES SINS: THE INSTITUTION OF THE SACRAMENT OF PENANCE

What do you think? If a shepherd has a hundred sheep, and one of
them has gone astray, does he not leave the ninety-nine on the moun-
tains and go in search of the one that went astray? And if he finds it,
truly I tell you, he rejoices over it more than over the ninety-nine
that never went astray. So it is not the will of your Father in heaven
that one of these little ones should be lost.

—Matthew 18:12–14

## THE BREATH OF FORGIVENESS

In John's Gospel, the Risen Lord "breathed on them and said to them,
'receive the holy Spirit. Whose sins you forgive are forgiven them,
and whose sins you retain are retained'" (John 20:22–23). There is thus
a linkage between the Risen Lord's breathing on them, the Holy Spirit
and the forgiveness of sins.

The sacrament we call reconciliation or penance was born in the
Upper Room on Easter Sunday night. It is a sacrament of divine mercy.
On Holy Thursday, in that same room, the sacraments of the Eucharist
and Holy Orders had been instituted. How blessed we are! Such power
going forth from the Body of Christ for all times from that Upper
Room!

About the institution of the sacrament of penance, the Council of
Trent (1551) teaches:

As a means of regaining grace and justice, penance was at all times
necessary for those who had defiled their souls with any mortal
sin.... Before the coming of Christ, penance was not a sacrament,

nor is it since his coming a sacrament for those who are not baptized. But the Lord then principally instituted the Sacrament of Penance, when, being raised from the dead, he breathed upon his disciples saying: "Receive ye the Holy Ghost. Whose sins you shall forgive, they are forgiven them; and whose sins you shall retain, they are retained" (John 20:2–23). By which action so signal and words so clear the consent of all the Fathers has ever understood that the power of forgiving and retaining sins was communicated to the Apostles and to their lawful successors, for the reconciling of the faithful who have fallen after Baptism.[32]

This moment in the Upper Room is a miracle and a mystery even greater than when God first breathed life into Adam, for this "breath" will undo the sin of Adam, the heritage of sin that is ours. The "yes" of Mary, the "New Eve," broke the power of the evil one that had orchestrated the downfall of our first parents. The surrender of Christ, the "New Adam," to the will of God ensured that all of creation would be returned to its former splendor. And all of it was brought about by the movement of the Spirit in the womb of the Blessed Mother.

By breathing the Spirit into that Upper Room, the Lord showed a new and mighty work of the Spirit: not only as the author of life, but as the healer and restorer as well. In the sacrament of penance, the priest prays: "God, the Father of mercies, through the death and resurrection of his Son has reconciled the world to himself and sent the Holy Spirit among us for the forgiveness of sins." Here we see the role of the Spirit in this healing sacrament: The Spirit convicts us of our sins—makes them known to us—and makes forgiveness and deep healing possible.

One of the cornerstones of Pope Francis's papacy has been an encouragement of this sacrament and highlighting the restorative power of God, that is, mercy. In fact, he called for an Extraordinary Jubilee Year of Mercy in 2015–16. In so doing, he reminds us that confession is not just about acknowledging our own wrongdoing; it is also about healing and reconciling souls to one another, about restoring relationships between ourselves as well as between ourselves and God.

## CONFESSION AND HEALING

At one of his daily homilies, Pope Francis offers reassuring words he has used often during his papacy about the sacrament of penance, which speaks of God's longing to restore us into relationship with him—a desire that manifested itself in the longing of Christ to spend that last Passover with his disciples in the Upper Room. Pope Francis declares:

> First of all, God always forgives us. He never tires of this. It's we who get tired of asking for forgiveness. But he does not tire of pardoning us. When Peter asked Jesus: "How many times must I forgive? Seven times?"—"Not seven times: seventy times by seven." Namely always. That's how God forgives us: always. But if you have lived a life full of so many sins, so many bad things, but in the end, a bit repentant, you ask for forgiveness, he will immediately pardon you! He always pardons us.[33]

I cannot emphasize enough, from my thirty years of priestly experience and from the similar wisdom of so many other priests, what an incredible joy it is to hear confessions, and in addition, to experience as a penitent the healing presence of Jesus. As a priest, it is a joy to seize the confessional experience as an opportunity to teach the faith and manifest a forgiving and merciful heart. Ample opportunities must be provided in our parishes. It can be a beautiful encounter of God's merciful love for both the priest and penitent.

But the priest cannot do it alone. Each baptized Catholic must encourage broad use of this sacrament of mercy. One of the spiritual works of mercy, after all, is to admonish the sinner. That means to encourage, as an act of love, one to refrain from falling into sin. It also means to encourage a sinner (and each one of us is a sinner) to experience the sacrament of reconciliation regularly. We can never tire of inviting people to come to confession.

This sacrament of mercy is a unique priestly opportunity to tailor the faith one-on-one to an individual penitent, typically with a short, spirit-filled exhortation, especially with regards to the challenging moral teachings of our faith. Confession is an opportunity, with the powerful assistance of the Holy Spirit, to explain our teachings in a kind way, to encourage, to assist, to forgive, and to allow Jesus to heal one-on-one through our priestly ministry. It is also one of the most effective means of personal growth in our search for holiness.

### CONFESSION AND TEACHING

Outside the confessional, teaching the ten commandments must be a significant part of the catechetical effort. Each of us is on the front lines of that movement. Each of us needs to be involved in this very important effort of teaching the faith to our spouses, our children, witnessing the faith to coworkers and members of our families, those who are part of our social life. It takes courage to walk in the footsteps of the Lord Jesus as priests and laity. Teaching the faith is a joint effort.

Not only does this teaching help individuals learn right from wrong, it also helps the broader society, complex as it is, learn to live together amicably. For those of us who are Catholics, it also provides a wonderful framework for our examination of conscience—so necessary in an appropriate celebration of the sacrament of penance.

I am told that the real reason individuals do not go to confession is not simply because they do not know or have forgotten the formula for the act of contrition (a common concern that any faithful priest is ready and willing to alleviate). The real problem is that far too many have *lost the understanding of right from wrong.* The ten commandments are an excellent way to help individuals examine their consciences, or even *form* their consciences. They are an important key to the New Evangelization.

The New Evangelization is the Church's present effort to re-propose the eternal verities of our faith in a way that fills in the huge gaps of an increasingly secular society. There is an urgency in this effort in our time. Through it, the Church strives to make the sacrament of confession more desirable and less a cause of anxiety. Instead of viewing confession as a burden of religiosity, we should see it as a gift. Through this sacrament, we can be certain of the forgiveness of our sins by encountering the healing Jesus in the person of the priest in confession.

We can never doubt, moreover, that the forgiveness of sins is a fundamental creedal principle of our faith. Jesus has already paid for our sins by his death and glorious resurrection. This is a teaching about hope, true and lasting hope, and above all, a teaching about God's continual mercy. Or as Pope Francis emphasizes, "Among the sacraments, the Sacrament of Reconciliation certainly renders present the merciful face of God with special efficacy."[34]

### RECEIVING HIM IN YOUR UPPER ROOM

The institution of the sacrament of reconciliation, like the Eucharist and Holy Orders, took place in the Upper Room. This sacrament is a significant gift of the Upper Room. The graces of mercy and forgiveness are a part of that steady manifestation of the Lord's merciful love for us from the moment of his resurrection.

As I wrote about this sacrament in one of my other books, "The sacrament of Penance is extremely personal. Sins cannot be faxed, e-mailed, or delivered by FedEx. A number of years ago, speaking to

French bishops, our late Holy Father John Paul II said this about the sacrament of Penance: 'At a period in which private life is extolled and people wish to protect it against the pressures and the anonymity of large human groups, the act of confessing one's sins and receiving from God a word of forgiveness addressed personally to each individual is to proclaim that, in the human race, each one counts before God.'"[35]

# CHAPTER TEN

# Jesus—the Face of the Father's Loving Mercy

But God, who is rich in mercy, because of the great love he had for us, even when we were dead in our transgressions, brought us to life with Christ.

—Ephesians 2:4–5

## His Father's Mercy

Throughout his entire life, Jesus was a mirror of his Father's mercy, the Father who is "rich in mercy." Jesus not only speaks of mercy. He himself is mercy. Stated differently, he is the definitive revelation of the Father's mercy, so the Father is never forgotten—only explicated and explained in and through Jesus Christ. In other words, "To see Jesus is to see the Father" (*DV* 4).

If Jesus were physically walking among us today (and we know he is living within each and every one of us), he would say that just as he acts, so too does his Father act. In the words of St. Paul's Letter to Titus, he writes:

> But when the kindness and generous love of God our savior appeared, not because of any righteous deeds we had done but because of his mercy, he saved us through the bath of rebirth and renewal by the holy Spirit, whom he richly poured out on us through Jesus Christ our savior, so that we might be justified by his grace and become heirs in hope of eternal life. (Titus 3:4–7)

Jesus is the merciful face of his Father. It is his mercy that saves us—not our own actions or words. It is through his mercy that we were given the gift of the Holy Spirit, so that we would never be alone, as Jesus promised that night in the Upper Room.

How do we see the merciful face of the Father in Jesus Christ? Where do we look? I look to the magnificent Vatican Council document *Dei Verbum* ("On Divine Revelation") for an answer. The Council, speaking on how Jesus completed and perfected Revelation, wrote:

> He did this by the total fact of his presence and self-manifestation—
> by words and works, signs and miracles, but above all by his death
> and glorious resurrection from the dead, and finally by sending the
> Spirit of truth. (*DV* 4)

So we look to the words and deeds of Jesus, which are "intrinsically bound up with one another" (*DV* 2). It is there that we see the mercy of the Father through the face of Jesus—his words and deeds.

To see more examples of his mercy, look at the many healings he performed, and above all, the cross as a citadel of his love and mercy for us. At its heart, mercy properly understood is the face of God's love as it makes contact with the sinner and triggers conversion and healing. Mercy comes first, encouraging conversion of heart. God's mercy impels the sinner along the path of conversion in every sacramental encounter. At Mass, before Holy Communion, the priest prays: "but through your loving mercy, be for me protection in mind and body and a healing remedy."

At the sacrament of penance, the priest, in absolving our sins, calls on "the Father of mercies, through the death and resurrection of his Son (who) has reconciled the world to himself and sent the Holy Spirit among us for the forgiveness of sins." In and through God's mercy, our sins are forgiven and we are healed.

If mercy is to have a face in our increasingly broken world, it will be through the mercy of God, in Jesus, unleashed in that sacramental encounter with him in and through each penitent. I write of each one of us, privileged to be the product of a conversion experience through his merciful glance and embrace.

## Miserando Atque Eligendo

God never gives up on his mercy, especially in our time where there exists the false perception of self-sufficiency and lack of awareness of one's very sinfulness. These joint heresies endanger souls by creating the erroneous perception so prevalent in this day and age: that we have no need for mercy. Nothing could be further from the truth—and yet, for those who are willing to concede their need, nothing is simpler to remedy. Mercy is his loving face directed to the healing of the wounds of sin, the wounds that trigger a separation and distance in our relationship with God.

This takes place in and through the Church, his living body. In fact, "the Church's very credibility is seen in how she shows merciful and compassionate love" (*MV* 10). Or as Pope Francis has said: "An inhospitable Church, just as a family shut-in on itself, mortifies the Gospel and hardens the world. No armour-plated doors in the Church, none! Everything open!"[36]

Jesus was the master of God's loving mercy for the many signs he worked. His miracles, especially in the face of sinners, the poor, the marginalized, the sick, and the suffering, were all meant to teach mercy. There are many examples of the loving mercy of Jesus in his public ministry. The first that comes to mind is the call of St. Matthew to be an apostle of Jesus (Matthew 9:9–13). In the Scripture text, we read simply that Jesus saw a man named Matthew at his customs post. Seeing him, he said to him—"Follow me." Scripture tells us that he got up and followed him without hesitation.

Now you might ask, where is the evidence of mercy in the calling of Matthew by Jesus? The medieval churchman, St. Bede the Venerable, commenting on this Gospel text, wrote: "Jesus looked upon Matthew with merciful love and chose him ("*miserando atque eligendo*," *MV* 8). He wrote that Jesus saw Matthew through the eyes of mercy. Matthew's acceptance was evidence of a conversion of sorts in the face of the merciful glance of Jesus. He abandoned his earthly wealth to follow Jesus immediately. "By an invisible, interior impulse flooding his mind with the light of grace, [Jesus] instructed him to walk in his footsteps," wrote St. Bede. "In this way Matthew could understand that Christ, who was summoning him away from earthly possessions, had incorruptible treasures of heaven in his gift." Matthew had a conversion experience, which is a significant part of a proper understanding of mercy's effect, and he displayed this by following Jesus and leaving his tax collector's stand.

Pope Francis writes that this expression, *miserando atque eligendo* ("because he saw him through eyes of mercy and chose him") impressed him so much that he chose it for his episcopal motto (*MV* 8). In fact, in Cuba on the feast of St. Matthew, in his homily, Pope Francis, speaking of the apostle Matthew, said:

> After the Lord looked upon him with mercy, he said to Matthew: "Follow me." Matthew got up and followed him. After the look, a word. After love, the mission. Matthew is no longer the same; he is changed inside. The encounter with Jesus and his loving mercy has transformed him. He leaves behind his table, his money, his exclusion. Before, he had sat waiting to collect his taxes, to take from others; now, with Jesus he must get up and give, give himself to others. Jesus looks at him and Matthew encounters the joy of service.[37]

Jesus Christ was and continues to be a God of compassionate healing and mercy. In fact, his entire ministry testifies to the healing mercy of our God. And the parables, especially the Merciful Father (otherwise known as the Prodigal Son) demonstrate so beautifully the forgiveness of sin as a continuing act of his healing mercy.

At a certain point in his ministry, however, the initial enthusiasm of the people for him experienced a reversal. He was criticized for doing good, for example, on the Sabbath and for forgiving sin. They said, "Why does this man speak that way? He is blaspheming. Who but God alone can forgive sins?" (Mark 2:7) That Jesus ate with tax collectors and sinners caused great scandal in his day. But it was his continual desire to heal them with his merciful love that attracted them to him. That was, and is, at the core of the Gospel—reaching out to those on the periphery of society—those most in need of God's merciful love.

Ultimately, it was his very deeds of mercy that aroused opposition. His opponents regard these expressions of loving mercy—healing on the Sabbath, for example—as scandalous. In more ways than one, it was his mercy that brought him to Calvary and the great scandal of the cross.

The perennial question immediately arises as to how a merciful God can allow his Son to be crucified in such a brutal way? Short answer: Jesus accepts suffering, walks in our place, which truly is his final offer of mercy. At the Last Supper in the Upper Room, in his last will and testament, he affirms he is doing this, appropriating this suffering, for us: "This is my body, which will be given up for you." The "you" is you and I. Only God could deliver us from our deepest adversity, the affliction of death. His death is the death of death. Instead of death, he gives us a new and eternal life. In the words of St. Peter, "Blessed be the God and Father of our Lord Jesus Christ, who in his great mercy gave us a new birth to a living hope through the resurrection of Jesus Christ from the dead" (1 Peter 1:3).

What he did out of love, and mercy, is called a "substitutionary atonement," which liberates us for a new life and makes us a new creation.

Only God can do this. He alone effects our salvation, but not without our involvement. It involves us, as we have the opportunity in faith to say "yes" anew for the salvation won for us.

Importantly, the cross does not have the last word. His resurrection does. Without the resurrection, the cross would be a seal of failure. Instead the cross is a sign of victory. Cardinal Kasper writes in his book *Mercy:* "It is a sign of victory that says to us that love conquers over hate, life conquers over death, and that, in the end, mercy triumphs over judgment."[38] It creates a space for new life and freedom. Love conquers. For, "By his wounds, we are healed" (see Isaiah 53:5; 1 Peter 2:24). Cardinal Kasper sums up the death and resurrection of Jesus Christ and its effect this way: "To believe in the crucified son is to believe that love is present in the world and that it is more powerful than hate and violence, more powerful than all the evil in which human beings are entangled. 'Believing in this love means believing in mercy.'"[39]

Jesus Christ, in his entire ministry, on the cross, and through his resurrection is the face of the Father's mercy, a Father "rich in mercy" (Ephesians 2:4). To see him is to see his Father. As Pope Francis states in *Misericordiae Vultus*, "Jesus of Nazareth, by his words, his actions, and his entire person reveals the mercy of God" (*MV* 1).

## Receiving Him in Your Upper Room

In that beautiful sacrament of penance, that sacrament instituted in the Upper Room for you and me, the mercy of our God continues in our time. It is the merciful face of Jesus that he so wishes to unveil for each one of us, the merciful face of the Father's perduring love. To believe in love, a love more powerful than any and all evil, means believing and affirming the mercy of God.

Take some time to reflect on a few examples of Jesus's merciful ministry from Scripture. I have included the following texts for you, but there are, of course, many others. How is God's mercy displayed in these passages? Take some time to pray over these verses and ask God to reveal a new understanding of his mercy to you through them.

Matthew 9:35–36: "Jesus went around to all the towns and villages, teaching in their synagogues, proclaiming the gospel of the kingdom, and curing every disease and illness. At the sight of the crowds, his heart was moved with pity for them because they were troubled and abandoned, like sheep without a shepherd."

Matthew 14:13–14: "When Jesus heard of it, he withdrew in a boat to a deserted place by himself. The crowds heard of this and followed him on foot from their towns. When he disembarked and saw the vast crowd, his heart was moved with pity for them, and he cured their sick."

Matthew 15:32: "Jesus summoned his disciples and said, 'My heart is moved with pity for the crowd, for they have been with me now for three days and have nothing to eat. I do not want to send them away hungry, for fear they may collapse on the way.'" And with just a few loaves of bread he satisfied the enormous crowd.

Matthew 18:26–27: "At that, the servant fell down, did him homage, and said, 'Be patient with me, and I will pay you back in full.' Moved with compassion the master of that servant let him go and forgave him the loan."

Matthew 20:32–34: "Jesus stopped and called them and said, 'What do you want me to do for you?' They answered him, 'Lord, let our eyes be opened.' Moved with pity, Jesus touched their eyes. Immediately they received their sight, and followed him."

Mark 1:40–41: "A leper came to him and kneeling down begged him and said, 'If you wish, you can make me clean.' Moved with pity, he stretched out his hand, touched him, and said to him, 'I do will it. Be made clean.'"

Mark 5:19: After Jesus freed the demoniac in the country of the Gerasenes, he entrusted him with this specific mission: "Go home to your family, and announce to them all the Lord in his pity has done for you."

Luke 7:12–14: "As he drew near to the gate of the city [called Naim], a man who had died was being carried out, the only son of his mother, and she was a widow. A large crowd from the city was with her. When the Lord saw her, he was moved with pity for her and said to her 'Do not weep.' he stepped forward and touched the coffin; at this the bearers halted, and he said, 'Young man, I tell you, arise!"

# CHAPTER ELEVEN

# THOMAS'S PROFESSION OF FAITH

It was not by chance but in God's providence [that Thomas was absent]. In a marvelous way God's mercy arranged that the disbelieving disciple [a week later], in touching the wounds of his master's body, should heal our wounds of disbelief. The disbelief of Thomas has done more for our faith than the faith of the other disciples. As he touches Christ and is won over to belief, every doubt is cast aside and our faith is strengthened. So the disciple who doubted, then felt Christ's wounds, becomes a witness to the reality of the resurrection.

—Pope St. Gregory the Great

## A WOUND WE SHARE

In addition to the coming of the Holy Spirit and the forgiveness of sins in the sacrament of penance set forth in John 20:24–25, we witness a crucial moment with Thomas. He was one of the apostles who was *not* present in the Upper Room when the Risen Lord came and breathed the Holy Spirit upon them on that first Easter Sunday night. When later told by the others that they had seen the Lord, he replied in that well-known response: "Unless I see the mark of the nails in his hands and put my finger into the nailmarks and put my hand into his side, I will not believe" (John 20:25).

Traditionally, he is called "Doubting Thomas." Yet *doubt* is a wound that each of us shares. It is not necessarily a fatal wound, nor is it a flat-out rejection of our faith. I can picture myself that evening having a similar doubt. Maybe you can as well. We certainly have experienced doubt in our efforts to explain the faith to others. Sometimes we are rejected. More often, we have to unveil the beauty of our faith over time and with utmost patience.

One of the great challenges of those of us in the "faith business"—and not one of us is excluded—is a challenge as old as the early days of the Church itself. I am thinking of St. Paul and his famous "Men of Athens" speech forever memorialized in Acts 17:22–31. He was speaking to the lawyers, judges and philosophers of his day—referring to them as a "religious people." Although none of them knew the person of Jesus, Paul understood the innate capacity for God in each of us. Still, he failed to make many converts that day. Most walked away. Each of us has had similar experiences in our lives. But Thomas teaches us that doubt is not the end of the story.

A week after his first Easter night appearance, the Risen Lord appeared once again in that same Upper Room. Scripture gives us an intimate view of that moment:

> Now a week later his disciples were again inside and Thomas was with them. Jesus came, although the doors were locked, and stood in their midst and said, "Peace be with you." Then he said to Thomas, "Put your finger here and see my hands, and bring your hand and put it into my side, and do not be unbelieving, but believe." Thomas answered and said to him, "My Lord and my God!" Jesus said to him, "Have you come to believe because you have seen me? Blessed are those who have not seen and have believed" (John 20:26–29).

This time, something happened to Thomas. He made a wonderful confession of Easter faith, an example for each of us: "My Lord and my God." The Lord's transforming presence and his words of peace changed Thomas's life. "Peace be with you."

The truth of the Resurrection had at last penetrated his heart, and healed his wounds of doubt. Pope Francis teaches:

With patience, Jesus does not abandon Thomas in his stubborn unbelief.... He does not close the door, he waits. And Thomas acknowledges his own poverty, his little faith. "My Lord and my God!": with this simple yet faith-filled invocation, he responds to Jesus' patience. He lets himself be enveloped by Divine Mercy; he sees it before his eyes, in the wounds of Christ's hands and feet and in his open side, and he discovers trust."[40]

God did not abandon Thomas in his doubt, nor does he abandon us. Our God, after all, is full of compassion and patience. Doubt is a wound we all share. It is a wound that God longs to heal with his divine mercy.

### HEALING THE WOUNDS OF DOUBT

We, like the apostle Thomas, have doubts from time to time. We are challenged to examine our faith with use of our reason and under the guidance of the Holy Spirit. Just as Thomas found faith and confessed it with the now famous words, "My Lord and my God," as a result of his personal encounter with the Risen One, so do we strengthen our faith and deal with our doubts each time we encounter him. That takes place when we gather for Mass. We encounter him when we receive the Risen Christ in Holy Communion, when we hear the inspired and Spirit-filled words of the Risen Christ in the readings, and when we share this experience at Mass with each other.

Importantly, faith requires perseverance. It often grows in stages. Sometimes we fall. Sometimes we walk away. So often, we must crawl. It seems that so often our faith must stand the test of perils and even scandal. We know this from our personal experience and from the experiences of the global Church. But we are not lone rangers: "To live, grow, and persevere in the faith until the end we must nourish it with the word of God; we must beg the Lord to increase our faith; it must be 'working through charity,' abounding in hope, and rooted in the faith of the Church" (*CCC* 162). The Church's faith, the faith that has perdured and developed over the centuries, precedes, engenders, supports, and nourishes our faith.

If we listen carefully, we can hear the Risen Lord speaking directly to each of us in Thomas's story when he says, "Blessed are those who have not seen and have believed." There are periods of doubt in each follower of Jesus. For some, there may even be periods of inactivity in the faith. But with God's grace, our faith returns through his divine mercy—for he is full of mercy and compassion. He always seeks us out.

Pope Francis emphasizes, "Our faith is not an abstract doctrine or philosophy, but a vital and full relationship with a person: Jesus Christ, the only-begotten Son of God who became man, was put to death, rose from the dead to save us, and is now living in our midst."[41] Faith is a response to our living God. Faith is both a free human act and, at the same time, an impulse of the Holy Spirit. Both are required.

Whether we consciously admit to it or not, our faith—our life in Christ—has sustained us throughout the ups and downs of our lives. It has sustained us in moments of new life and in death, at times of sickness, and at those times when we struggle to give meaning to painful situations.

We believe because the Lord Jesus has first seen us, singled us out, and breathed on us his life-giving Spirit, the Spirit of Risen Life, as he did to the apostles in the Upper Room on that Easter Sunday night. He gave us the Eucharist in that same Upper Room and guided us in ways of holiness. He continues to heal us in the sacrament of reconciliation, where we share in the restorative power of God.

## RECEIVING HIM IN YOUR UPPER ROOM

Not only does God close the wounds of Jesus in raising him from the dead, but Jesus closes the wounds of his apostles in the Upper Room, particularly the wounds of Thomas's doubt. He also heals our wounds of disbelief with words of life. That is the direct and lasting effect of the Easter proclamation: "He is risen as he promised. Alleluia, alleluia!"

We turn in prayer to Mary, Mother of Mercy, in the beautiful words of the Magnificat (Luke 1:46–55):

> And Mary said:
> "My soul proclaims the greatness of the Lord;
> > my spirit rejoices in God my savior.
> For he has looked upon his handmaid's lowliness;
> > behold, from now on will all ages call me blessed.
> The Mighty One has done great things for me,
> > and holy is his name.
> His mercy is from age to age
> > to those who fear him.
> He has shown might with his arm,
> > dispersed the arrogant of mind and heart.
> He has thrown down the rulers from their thrones
> > but lifted up the lowly.
> The hungry he has filled with good things,
> > the rich he has sent away empty.
> He has helped Israel his servant,
> > remembering his mercy,
> according to his promise to our fathers,
> > to Abraham and to his descendants forever."

# PART THREE

# The Upper Room—
# Pentecost and its Effects

El Greco (Doménikos Theotokópoulos), *The Coming of the Holy Spirit*,
1596.Museo del Prado, Madrid, Spain.

In this the final part of the book, we look to the Upper Room as the birth chamber of the infant Church, where the disciples and Mary gathered for prayer and witnessed the power of God through the blazing presence of the Advocate the Lord had promised.

On his 2014 pilgrimage to the Holy Land, Pope Francis spoke of the Upper Room in this context, reminding us that this visitation of the Holy Spirit has implications not just for the apostles, but for each of us as well.

> The Upper Room reminds us of the birth of the new family, the Church, established by the risen Jesus; a family that has a Mother, the Virgin Mary. Christian families belong to this great family, and in it they find the light and strength to press on and be renewed, amid the challenges and difficulties of life. All God's children, of every people and language, are invited and called to be part of this great family, as brothers and sisters and sons and daughters of the one Father in heaven.
>
> These horizons are opened up by the Upper Room, the horizons of the Risen Lord and his Church. From here the Church goes forth, impelled by the life-giving breath of the Spirit. Gathered in prayer with the Mother of Jesus, the Church lives in constant expectation of a renewed outpouring of the Holy Spirit. Send forth your Spirit, Lord, and renew the face of the earth (cf. Ps 104:30).[42]

# CHAPTER TWELVE

# MARY IN THE UPPER ROOM— PRAYING FOR THE HOLY SPIRIT

With the Holy Spirit, Mary is always present in the midst of the people. She joined the disciples in praying for the coming of the Holy Spirit (Acts 1:14) and thus made possible the missionary outburst which took place at Pentecost. She is the Mother of the Church which evangelizes, and without her we could never truly understand the spirit of the new evangelization.

—Pope Francis, *Evangelii Gaudium, 284*

### THE PRESENCE OF MARY

After the Resurrection of Jesus, his post-Resurrection appear-ances, and the Ascension, the disciples returned to Jerusalem and "when they entered the city they went to the upper room where they were staying" (Acts 1:13). It was the same Upper Room to which we have referred throughout this book. This is where the apostles typically stayed when they were in Jerusalem.

In addition to the apostles, St. Luke explicitly states that "some women, and Mary the mother of Jesus, and his brothers" were also present in that Upper Room and they "devoted themselves with one accord to prayer" (Acts 1:14). Although Mary's presence in the Upper Room was only briefly mentioned in Acts, her presence has a very rich content in the history of salvation. Mary and the disciples prepared prayerfully there for a new coming and outpouring of the Holy Spirit that would lead to the worldwide spread of the Gospel message.

In this chapter, our focus is, above all, on Mary, our Blessed Mother. It is about her presence and example in the Upper Room, the role of the Holy Spirit in her life, and the role of the Spirit in the Church from the day of Pentecost. Mary's presence and role was purposeful and intentional in God's plan for our salvation. As we have seen, "after her Son's Ascension, Mary 'aided the beginnings of the Church by her prayers.' In her association with the apostles and several women, 'we also see Mary by her prayers imploring the gift of the Spirit, who had already overshadowed her in the Annunciation'" (CCC 965).

### BEFORE THE UPPER ROOM

This Upper Room experience was not Mary's first encounter with the Holy Spirit. The prelude to this story, where it all began, was the movement of grace at the Annunciation, which enabled her to say, "May it be done to me according to your word" (Luke 1:38). The angel had announced that Mary would conceive a Son and name him Jesus, though she had had "no relations with a man," and declared: "The holy Spirit will come upon you, and the power of the Most High will overshadow you" (Luke 1:35). The Fathers of the Church teach, moreover, that Mary "conceived in her mind before she conceived him in her womb: precisely in faith" (RM 13).[43]

Her "may it be done to me" at Nazareth was a prayerful act of faith. In her act of prayer, she was fully open to the transforming power of the Holy Spirit. In fact, she was inwardly seized by the life-giving power of the Holy Spirit. It was the beginning of her journey of faith, a journey through the history of individuals and peoples that would ultimately begin for the entire Church in the Upper Room at Pentecost in her presence.

Our respective journeys of faith are also journeys in the power of the Holy Spirit, for "where the Spirit of the Lord is, there is freedom" (2 Corinthians 3:17). After her example, we also yield to the power of the Holy Spirit in our prayer lives and increasingly live as free men and women. Mary is always our model of faith.

St. John Paul II teaches about Mary:

> In a sense her journey of faith is longer. The Holy Spirit had already come down upon her, and she became his faithful spouse at the Annunciation, welcoming the Word of the true God…indeed abandoning herself totally to God through "the obedience of faith."…
> The journey of faith made by Mary, whom we see praying in the Upper Room, is thus longer than that of the others gathered there: Mary "goes before them," "leads the way" for them.[44]

Then, as if to sum up Mary's indispensable role, St. John Paul II states that "the moment of Pentecost in Jerusalem had been prepared for by the moment of the Annunciation in Nazareth, as well as by the Cross. In the Upper Room Mary's journey meets the Church's journey of faith" and she leads the way for each of us.[45]

And why was this? "…since it had pleased God not to manifest solemnly the mystery of the salvation of the human race before he would pour forth the Spirit promised by Christ."[46] It is for that reason that "we see the apostles before the day of Pentecost 'persevering with one mind in prayer with the women and Mary the Mother of Jesus, and with his brethren" (Acts 1:14).

## ROOM FOR PRAYER

As we have seen at the Last Supper, the Upper Room was a "room of prayer," where we listened to the prayer of Jesus to his Father the night before he died. Now we read of the prayer of Mary and the apostles in anticipation of the coming of the Holy Spirit at Pentecost. The Upper Room is another name for prayer itself, as it can be realized in the upper rooms of our daily lives. To this very day, more intense prayer, after the example of Mary and the apostles in the Upper Room, is likewise an integral part of the preparation for the receiving of the strength and graces of the Holy Spirit at confirmation (*CCC* 1310) and at every important moment of our lives. And the Holy Spirit is the breath of prayer, and the Holy Spirit sets us free in the Lord Jesus.

Prayer is an experience of meeting God, a lived and living encounter with God. It is an integral part of developing a friendship with him. Prayer is not simply talking to God. He knows our every thought and desire. Prayer, above all, is *listening* to God, listening to him from the quiet of our hearts. Prayer is listening *for* God. And that requires silence—a nearly forgotten part of our contemporary American life.

It is tempting to value the *answer* to our prayers over prayer itself. Sometimes, we await the answer to our prayers, our desired answer, and seemingly fail to receive it. Other times we receive our answer to prayer that was our hope in a different way. Over time we come to see his wisdom for us even when it is different from what we expected. But it is the act of prayer itself that unites us with God—not the answers he does or does not offer.

Prayer, which leads to friendship with God, means also walking with him, simply being in his presence, shutting everything else out of our minds. Prayer means embracing silence. It is not unlike spending quiet, uneventful time with someone you love. Prayer is touching him, allowing him to touch us. It is a conscious awareness of his presence, an intimacy with him, a daily appointment.

We are told to pray constantly (1 Thessalonians 5:17). Prayer is both gift and duty. Only in and through the Holy Spirit are we in fact able to pray. Prayer is akin to oxygen. It energizes us and makes true discipleship possible.

St. Josemaria Escriva once wrote that the first appointment every day should be with Jesus Christ. That appointment is a prayerful encounter of friendship. It affects the rest of the day when we begin faithfully in the prayerful presence of God in the upper rooms of our lives.

When we focus on Mary in the Upper Room before Pentecost with the apostles, devoting "themselves with one accord to prayer," her role and model as a woman of prayer is important for us to remember and imitate. It helps define her and our relationship with her. Mary always leads us to her Son. Her prayerful example is instructive in our personal lives as we, too, continually call upon the Holy Spirit to guide and energize us in our Christian lives and charitable outreach.

The *Catechism of the Catholic Church* teaches:

> Before the incarnation of the Son of God, and before the outpouring of the Holy Spirit, her prayer cooperates in a unique way with the Father's plan of loving kindness: at the Annunciation, for Christ's conception; at Pentecost, for the formation of the Church, his Body. In the faith of his humble handmaid, the Gift of God found the acceptance he had awaited from the beginning of time. She whom the Almighty made "full of grace" responds by offering her whole being: "Behold I am the handmaid of the Lord; let it be [done] to me according to your word." (*CCC* 2617)

The first time the Holy Spirit overshadowed Mary, she gave birth to the Lord Jesus. When the Holy Spirit at Pentecost rests on those in the Upper Room, including Mary, the Church is born. Mary's prayerful presence in the Upper Room in preparation for the Holy Spirit at Pentecost has, if you will, a special significance, precisely because of her prior bond with the Holy Spirit from the moment of the Incarnation. As if to underscore the importance of Mary's role at the Annunciation and Pentecost, St. Luke is the author of both accounts—in his Gospel (the Annunciation) and in the Acts of the Apostles (Pentecost).

There is much more to the story about Mary's faith and its relationship to the apostles in the Upper Room, that special group who received from the Risen One the unique mission to go forth and teach all nations. St. John Paul II teaches that Mary "... was present among them as an exceptional witness to the mystery of Christ...when the Church 'enters more intimately into the supreme mystery of the Incarnation,' she thinks of the Mother of Christ with profound reverence and devotion. ...It is precisely Mary's faith which marks the beginning of the new and eternal Covenant of God with man in Jesus Christ."[47] And this "Heroic faith of hers 'precedes' the apostolic witness of the Church, and ever remains in the Church's heart hidden like a special heritage of God's revelation. All those who from generation to generation accept the apostolic witness of the Church share in that mysterious inheritance, and in a sense share in Mary's faith."[48]

We are thus reminded from her prayerful presence in the Upper Room that Mary importantly and uniquely "leads the way" of the apostles who were praying with her and that her faith "precedes" the apostolic witness and mission given uniquely to the apostles. St. John Paul II reminds us, however, that unlike the apostles "Mary did not directly receive this apostolic mission. She was not among those whom Jesus sent 'to the whole world to teach all nations' (cf. Matthew 28:19) when he conferred this mission on them."[49]

By no means, however, does her lack of receipt of the apostolic mission minimize her essential and unique role in salvation history. In fact, she has been hailed by the Second Vatican Council as "preeminent and as a wholly unique member of the Church" (LG 53). Mary was, after all, in the same Upper Room with the apostles. We read, "And that first group of those who in faith looked 'upon Jesus as the author of salvation,' knew that Jesus was the Son of Mary, and that she was his Mother, and that as such she was from the moment of his conception and birth a unique witness to the mystery of Jesus, that mystery which before their eyes had been disclosed and confirmed in the Cross and Resurrection."[50]

From that time, then, those gathered in the Upper Room, and those who would follow them, looked upon Mary to Jesus, just as they would look at Jesus through the person of Mary, his mother. She always leads us to him, and she does this in the upper rooms of our daily lives, especially in all our humble efforts at prayer, prayer in the power of the Holy Spirit.

## Living the Upper Room

With her prayerful "*fiat*" (let it be), Mary became the first disciple after whom each of us should model our lives. She was the first disciple because it was her "yes" at the Annunciation that made possible the Incarnation of the Son of God and ultimately the birth of the Church, the body of Christ, in the power of the Holy Spirit at Pentecost.

You and I are called to say "yes" to Christ each and every day in our prayer as we seek to follow him. We are invited to read Luke 1:47–55 and meditate on Mary's prayerful "yes." What opportunity do you have to say "yes" to God in your life?

# CHAPTER THIRTEEN

# TONGUES OF FIRE AND THE COMING OF THE HOLY SPIRIT

The missions of the Son and the Holy Spirit are inseparable and constitute a single economy of salvation. The same Spirit who acts in the incarnation of the Word in the womb of the Virgin Mary is the Spirit who guides Jesus throughout his mission and is promised to the disciples. The same Spirit who spoke through the prophets sustains and inspires the Church in her task of proclaiming the word of God and in the preaching of the Apostles; finally, it is this Spirit who inspires the authors of sacred Scripture.[51]

—Pope Benedict XVI, *Verbum Domini*, 15

## THE PROMISED ADVOCATE

The story of the Upper Room is not yet finished. The prayers of those gathered at Pentecost were finally answered. The Church was about to be born, a Church called to energize the world until the end of time.

It was Pentecost, fifty days after Easter, according to St. Luke in the Acts of the Apostles. That day was a momentous one, for "On that day, [in the Upper Room] the Holy Trinity is fully revealed" (*CCC* 732). The Holy Spirit had been revealed gradually, and was the last of the Persons of the Trinity to be revealed, although the Spirit has from the beginning been a part of God's plan of salvation for us.

That day, though, the Spirit did not come quietly! We read: "And suddenly there came from the sky a noise like a strong driving wind, and it filled the entire house in which they were. Then there appeared to them tongues as of fire, which parted and came to rest on each one of them. And they were all filled with the holy Spirit and began to speak in different tongues, as the Spirit enabled them to proclaim" (Acts 2:2–4).

This "fullness" of the Spirit was unlike anything they had ever experienced before. The incredible sound that resulted from this experience must have spilled out into the street to the gathering crowd. Those gathered were confused because "each one heard them speaking in his own language" (Acts 2:6).

The Holy Spirit has often been described as the "forgotten person" of the Blessed Trinity even though we refer to the Holy Spirit in the creed we profess each Sunday: "I believe in the Holy Spirit, the Lord, the giver of life, who proceeds from the Father and the Son, who with the Father and the Son is adored and glorified, who has spoken through the prophets." And this has such important implications for each of us. St. Paul tells us that "No one can say, 'Jesus is Lord,' except by the holy Spirit" (1 Corinthians 12:3). St. John refers to the Holy Spirit as "rivers of living water" flowing from within a person who believes.

In the Upper Room, on the night before he died, Jesus kept telling his disciples that he had to leave them and would send them the Advocate, another name for the Holy Spirit. In fact, he told them, "But I tell you the truth, it is better for you that I go. For if I do not go, the Advocate will not come to you" (John 16:7). The Holy Spirit, fully revealed at Pentecost, comes to the apostles in the Upper Room only because of Jesus's departure.

## THE HOLY SPIRIT HAS COME!

How fortunate we are that the Holy Spirit came to Mary and the apostles and those gathered in the Upper Room. The Holy Spirit continues to come to each of us—first in baptism when we were baptized in one Spirit into one body, and then more fully in confirmation. The Spirit comes every time we pray for his varying gifts to us—gifts of wisdom, understanding, counsel, fortitude, knowledge, piety, and fear of the Lord. As Scripture tells us, "there are different kinds of spiritual gifts but the same Spirit…one and the same Spirit produces all of these, distributing them individually to each person as he wishes" (1 Corinthians 12:4,11).

It is the Holy Spirit that allows us to pray, to cry out *Abba, Father*. St. John Paul II referred to prayer itself as the "breath" of the Holy Spirit. That is why "… no one can say 'Jesus is Lord' except by the holy Spirit" (1 Corinthians 12:3).

This movement of the Holy Spirit happens in the upper rooms of our lives. It can happen each time we call upon the Holy Spirit. As Christians, each and every day we must call upon the Holy Spirit and not forget him. Pope Francis referred to the Holy Spirit as our "traveling companion."[52] Did you ever think of the presence of the Holy Spirit as akin to a traveling companion guiding us on our journey of life? The image of the Holy Spirit painted by those words is active and alive.

### The Holy Spirit Is Alive

The Holy Spirit is alive by grace in each of us and alive in the living body of Christ that is the Church. In fact, the Holy Spirit is the soul of the Church. Annually each year, when we celebrate Pentecost, the birthday of the Church, that day when the Holy Spirit was sent to Mary and those gathered in the Upper Room, we pray with special intensity: "Come Holy Spirit, Come!"

We pray each day for the coming anew of the Holy Spirit in our concrete lives. We pray that we might be more and more receptive to God's holy Word, remaining open, docile, and obedient, and that we will be transformed into him in the power and fire of the Holy Spirit.

The Holy Spirit is, after all, the new law of love. There is no way we could fully live the ten commandments, or the two great commandments, or the new commandment of love without the Holy Spirit within us. In fact, it was at Pentecost that the law of love was infused in the hearts of his disciples. In Romans 5:5, St. Paul teaches us that: "God's love has been poured into our hearts through the holy Spirit who has been given to us."

But how does this new law of the Spirit work? In effect, the Spirit gives us a new capacity for love. Living in grace, governed by the new law of the Spirit, is a way of living in love. It is not unlike falling in love with another person. It creates a new relationship. The Holy Spirit creates a loving relationship between us and God that we might be his full-time followers, each with an open heart that is capable of loving.

In addition, the Holy Spirit is the permanent gift of Easter—that glowing love of the Father and of the Son that has descended into our hearts. The Spirit now lives and is active in us. The Spirit helps us remember everything Christ has done and continues to do for us. Pope Francis reminds us that, "A Christian without memory is not a true Christian: he or she is a prisoner of circumstances." And it is the Holy Spirit, living in the Church today, who teaches us, each and every baptized person, how to enter into our history, into each and every encounter with Jesus, past and present.

Remember, it was at the Last Supper in the Upper Room, that Jesus promised his disciples that the Holy Spirit will teach them all things, reminding them of his words (cf. John 14:26). In so doing, the Spirit also helps us live the life of Jesus, his life of love, with courage and boldness, precisely because of his Spirit living and pulsating within us—the inexhaustible source of God's life within us.

With respect to Mary, the Holy Spirit came upon our Blessed Mother as early as her Annunciation. We read, "In Mary, the Holy Spirit *fulfills* the plan of the Father's loving goodness. Through the Holy Spirit, the

Virgin conceives and gives birth to the Son of God. By the Holy Spirit's power and her faith, her virginity became uniquely fruitful" (*CCC* 723). And there is more: "Mary belongs indissolubly to the mystery of Christ, and she belongs also to the mystery of the Church from the beginning, from the day of the Church's birth."[53] It was there in the Upper Room where Mary and the apostles devoted themselves to prayer. The promised Advocate, the Spirit of truth, thus came upon them, the Spirit promised the apostles in that same Upper Room on the night before Jesus died.

## LIVING THE UPPER ROOM

The Spirit comes gently, especially in our prayer. The Spirit is not felt as a burden, for the Spirit is light. The Spirit cannot be forced upon us. Instead, the Spirit comes with the tenderness of a true friend. The Spirit comes as a protector to save, to heal, to teach, to counsel, to strengthen, to console. In the words of St. Cyril of Jerusalem, "The Spirit comes to enlighten the mind first of the one who receives him, and then, through him, the minds of others as well."

# CHAPTER FOURTEEN

# FILLED WITH THE HOLY SPIRIT, THEY LEFT TO BECOME BOLD WITNESSES

From here (from the Upper Room) she set out, with the broken bread in her hands, the wounds of Christ before her eyes, and the Spirit of love in her heart. In the Upper Room, the risen Jesus, sent by the Father, bestowed upon the apostles his own Spirit and with this power he sent them forth to renew the face of the earth (cf. Psalm 104:30).

To go forth, to set out, does not mean to forget. The Church, in her going forth, preserves the memory of what took place here; the Spirit, the Paraclete, reminds her of every word and every action, and reveals their true meaning.

—Pope Francis, May 26, 2014

## ENTERPRISING, COURAGEOUS, AND BOLD

As we have seen, much happened in the Upper Room at Jerusalem. Everything that took place in that small room has permanently and positively affected our faith and the life of the Church down through the centuries until this very day. The Church continues to preserve the memory of the Upper Room. We have already looked at the Pentecost, and "the definitive manifestation of what had already been accomplished in the same Upper Room on Easter Sunday."[54] Now, we focus on the work of the Holy Spirit after Pentecost, the predicted "Spirit of truth" who has remained with us, as promised by Jesus, since that day.

Until now, the events of the Upper Room have taken place in private. But Pentecost changes everything. We see that, "What had then taken place inside the Upper Room, 'the doors being shut,' later, on the day of Pentecost is manifested also outside, in public. The doors of the

Upper Room are opened and the Apostles go to the inhabitants and the pilgrims who had gathered in Jerusalem on the occasion of the feast, in order to bear witness to Christ in the power of the Holy Spirit. In this way the prediction is fulfilled: 'he will bear witness to me: and you also are witnesses, because you have been with me from the beginning.'"[55]

Scripture tells us that great numbers of pilgrims had gathered in Jerusalem. Prompted and guided by the Holy Spirit, Peter and the others experienced a certain courage and "boldness" (Acts 4:13). Remember, this is the same Peter who had thrice denied Jesus, a denial predicted in the Upper Room, only weeks before. He was now a changed man, as were the other disciples. Or as Cardinal Wuerl writes: "The timid, shy, awkward, and fearful disciples suddenly became enterprising, courageous, bold proclaimers of the Gospel." [56]

On Pentecost, the disciples left the Upper Room, with spiritual toolboxes in hand, and attempted to put into practice what they had experienced and learned in the Upper Room. The Holy Spirit had empowered and changed them to be bold witnesses to the death and rising of Jesus. Even the way they acted and spoke had changed.

The Acts of the Apostles recounts what happened from Pentecost forward. In fact, the Acts of the Apostles has been called the Gospel of the Holy Spirit, so strong is the manifest influence and guidance of the Spirit in the early Church we see developing in the Acts. The disciples felt, over and over again, the full strength of the Holy Spirit, the Holy Spirit who is the soul of the Church and a lasting treasure in the life of the Church. It is a strength that is available to each of us if we are open to the movement of the Holy Spirit in our lives.

### THE BOLDNESS OF PETER

On Pentecost day, Peter powerfully proclaimed the death and resurrection of Jesus. He preached in the power of the Holy Spirit, and the crowds, also objects of the Spirit's activity, asked him what they were to do. Without any hesitation: "Peter [said] to them, 'repent and be baptized, every one of you, in the name of Jesus Christ for the forgiveness of your sins; and you will receive the gift of the holy Spirit'" (Acts 2:38).

Peter and the disciples had been charged to forgive sins in the Upper Room. That is precisely what Peter was doing on that first Pentecost. Scripture tells us that three thousand were baptized that very day and their sins forgiven. The call to repentance was at the very heart of the ministry of Jesus. He used the exact same word as Peter did on Pentecost when he began his public ministry: "Repent..." (Mark 1:15). Over and over again, Jesus demonstrated that "...mercy (the restorative power of God) is the very foundation of the Church's life."[57] It is the Holy Spirit who convicts us of our sins and acts like a healing balm.

As the Church began to grow, guided by the Holy Spirit in response to the strong witness of Peter and the apostles, events that took place in the privacy of the Upper Room once again became public. Under the guidance of the apostles, prayer, the institution of the Eucharist, acts of service, and fellowship became the core of the Christian message. Acts tells us that "they devoted themselves to the teaching of the apostles and to the communal life, to the breaking of the bread and to the prayers" (Acts 2:42).

The breaking of bread became a way of life in the early Church for Acts tells us that "every day they devoted themselves to meeting together in the temple area and to breaking bread in their homes.... And every day the Lord added to their number those who were being saved" (Acts 2:46–47). First, the Upper Room was a place of prayer and where the apostles broke bread with the Lord. Now, through their ministry, empowered by the Holy Spirit, those experiences continued in the early Church and continue in the upper rooms of our lives.

Healings also took place in the early Church. We see in the story of the crippled beggar, "Peter took him by the right hand and raised him up, and immediately his feet and ankles grew strong" (Acts 3:7). Pointing to the faith of the man healed, Peter told the crowds, as if to underscore a deeper healing possible for them: "Repent, therefore, and be converted, that your sins may be wiped away, and that the Lord may grant you times of refreshment and send you the Messiah already appointed for you, Jesus" (Acts 3:19–20). The gift of healing, along with the forgiveness of sins, was an essential gift of the Upper Room. These gifts spread, through Peter and the apostles, as the early Church grew and developed.

### Enduring through Persecution

Despite his newfound boldness, not all was easy for Peter and the apostles in the early days of the Church. The disciples were repeatedly warned by the authorities to stop teaching in Jesus's name. They were threatened, beaten, and imprisoned, but they persevered in their witness. When challenged, the answer of Peter and John was simply: "It is impossible for us not to speak about what we have seen and heard" (Acts 4:20). And they continued to speak and give faithful and bold witness. What incredible examples of faith for each of us!

We learn that the life of the early community of believers was "of one heart and mind" (Acts 4:32). There was not a needy person among them "for those who owned property or houses would sell them, bring the proceeds of the sale, and put them at the feet of the apostles, and they were distributed to each according to need" (Acts 4:34–35). By placing the proceeds of the sale of property at the feet of the apostles for those in need, the early Church was living out the example of service set by Jesus when he washed the feet of his disciples in the Upper Room. Christ's example, as followed by those earliest Christians, is one we, too, must strive to follow.

### Living the Upper Room

You and I are challenged to possess the same missionary resourceful-ness of the apostles in our age as a result of what happened in the Upper Room ages ago. There is no need to hide in the upper rooms of our lives out of fear or selfishness. We are missionary disciples on a perma-nent mission and, as such, called to allow the Holy Spirit to lead us as the Spirit led and empowered Peter and the apostles in the early days of the Church. What happened to them was not only a phenomenon for first-century Christians. It is also our legacy as privileged men and women, baptized into the Risen Lord. The Upper Room is an icon of a fruitful Church and its fruitfulness continues in and through each and every believer.

Like that early community of believers, we have the Eucharist as "the source and summit" of our lives, feeding us and strengthening us in our sacrificial love for one another. Pope Francis writes: "By his taking flesh and coming among us, Jesus has touched us, and through the sacra-ments he continues to touch us even today; transforming our hearts, he unceasingly enables us to acknowledge and acclaim him as the Son of God. In faith, we can touch him and receive the power of his grace."[58] What a gift!

Like the apostles, you and I are called in our day to heal and forgive—to forgive seven times seventy times. We are challenged to experience ever anew the knowledge of our salvation by the forgiveness of our sins, and to help others to come to that same knowledge.

The sacrament of mercy, the healing sacrament of reconciliation that was instituted in the Upper Room, continues to be a wonderful oasis of mercy in our day. In the sacrament of penance, the priest prays: "God, the Father of mercies, through the death and resurrection of his Son has reconciled the world to himself and sent the Holy Spirit among us for the forgiveness of sins." It is through the Holy Spirit that we know God's mercy, and in turn we must be ambassadors of mercy.

As Pope Francis wrote in *Misericordiae Vultus* (the Bull of Indiction of the Extraordinary Jubilee of Mercy): "In the present day, as the Church is charged with the task of the new evangelization, the theme of mercy needs to be proposed again and again with new enthusiasm and renewed pastoral action."[59] He said further that we should "place the sacrament of Reconciliation at the centre once more in such a way that it will enable people to touch the grandeur of God's mercy with their own hands."[60]

We are challenged daily to live lives of sacrificial love after the example of Jesus in the Upper Room in his washing the feet of the apostles. By washing their feet, Jesus became like a humble slave. In so many big and little ways, the challenge to follow the Upper Room Jesus in his servant-like example presents itself to us on a daily basis. We are called to reach out and share our loving heart with those in need and with those who seek the face of mercy.

We receive the fullness of the Holy Spirit in the sacrament of confirmation and are challenged to become more and more aware of the presence of the Holy Spirit within us. We are challenged to allow the Holy Spirit to guide us and take us out of our comfort zones, yielding to the movement of the Spirit in our daily lives and decisions. There is a boldness and an inner strength infused in us by the power of the Holy Spirit.

As we seek to follow the great commission and missionary mandate to go forth and make disciples of all nations in our day, we are fortunate heirs of the great gifts of the Upper Room—the Eucharist, Holy Orders, reconciliation, the example of loving service and prayer, the witness of faith, the maternal role of our Blessed Mother, and the powerful guidance and assistance of the Holy Spirit. We read, "Indeed, 'today missionary activity still represents the greatest challenge for the Church' and 'the missionary task must remain foremost.'" What would happen if we were to take these words seriously? We would realize that missionary outreach is paradigmatic for all the Church's activity."[61]

Speaking of the early disciples, and using St. Junipero Serra as an example from our continent, Pope Francis said:

> These missionary disciples who have encountered Jesus, the Son of God, who have come to know him through his merciful Father, moved by the grace of the Holy Spirit, went out to all the geographical, social and existential peripheries, to bear witness to charity. They challenge us![62]

Indeed, we are challenged by their example. Not unlike Peter and the other apostles, each and every believer is vested with the same Holy Spirit and the gifts of the Upper Room, in our own unique and personal ways. Empowered by the Spirit, we seek to be daily missionaries in our secular age. What has been handed down to us is clearly all we need to be true men and women of the new evangelization. We, too, have benefited—and continue to benefit—from the Upper Room.

Each one of us, with our own individual charisms, is called to be a witness of the faith. That witness takes on many forms and has many faces. Some are catechists, others are teachers of the faith, whether from the pulpit, in the classroom or in a parish setting, or in our families. Each of us, then, has a role in passing on the faith by means of helping to bring others, and ourselves, into deeper touch with the Person of Jesus Christ. It is not simply a job. It is a vocation and a way of life. It is an art and a gift of the Holy Spirit.

How blessed then are we! Praised be Jesus Christ, our Lord and Savior, for he has risen as he promised and continues to live. We know that "In faith, we can touch him and receive the power of his grace."[63]

This we can powerfully do, after the example of St. Peter and the others in that Upper Room, in the upper rooms of our own lives. We can do this because of what happened millennia ago in a particular place in history called the Upper Room, or Cenacle, in Jerusalem. What happened there was and continues to be a fruitful icon of the Church, God's holy people, all in the power of the Holy Spirit.

## ACKNOWLEDGMENTS

With gratitude to my Archbishop, Cardinal Donald Wuerl, my editor, Heidi Saxton, and to Fr. Patrick Lewis, Father George Stuart, Elizabeth Meers, and Kathleen Pomerenk for their kind assistance.

# NOTES

1.  Pope Francis, homily, May 26, 2014.

2.  Pope Francis, homily, May 26, 2014.

3.  Pope Benedict XVI, *Jesus of Nazareth: Holy Week,* vol. II (San Francisco: Ignatius, 2011), 115.

4.  Pope Benedict XVI, *Jesus of Nazareth,* 119.

5.  Pope Francis, homily, May 30, 2013.

6.  Pope Benedict XVI, homily, May 22, 2008.

7.  The Gospel accounts of this story are found in Matthew 26:20–25; Mark 14:17–21; Luke 22:14–23; and John 13:21–26.

8.  Jean Galot, *The Eucharistic Heart* (San Francisco: Ignatius, 1990), 41.

9.  Pope Francis, homily, April 7, 2013.

10. Chris Lowney, *Pope Francis: Why He Leads the Way He Leads* (Chicago: Loyola, 2013), 41.

11. Pope Francis, homily, May 26, 2014.

12. Gerhard Lohfink. *Jesus of Nazareth: What He Wanted, Who He Was* (Collegeville, MN.: Michael Glazier, 2015), 75.

13. James Martin, SJ, *Jesus: A Pilgrimage* (New York: HarperOne, 2016), 345.

14. Pope Francis. "Message of His Holiness Pope Francis for Lent 2015," https://w2.vatican.va/content/francesco/en/messages/lent/documents/papa-francesco_20141004_messaggio-quaresima2015.html.

15. Pope John Paul II, "To Priests," https://w2.vatican.va/content/john-paul-ii/en/letters/1998/documents/hf_jp-ii_let_31031998_priests.html.

16. Galot, 130.

17. Pope Francis. "Memory and service," https://w2.vatican.va/content/francesco/en/cotidie/2015/documents/papa-francesco-cotidie_20150430_memory-and-service.html.

18. *Evangelii Gaudium*, 203.

19. *Centesimus Annus,* 11.

20. *Mater et Magistra*, 218.

21. *Mater et Magistra,* 219.

22. *Mater et Magistra,* 220.

23. *Gaudium et Spes,* 22, 2.

24. Zenit staff, "Pope Francis' Addresses and Homilies During Visit to Roman Parish of Regina Pacis," *ZENIT,* May 4, 2015, https://zenit.org/articles/pope-francis-addresses-and-homilies-during-visit-to-roman-parish-of-regina-pacis/.

25. Pope Francis, "The nameless man," https://w2.vatican.va/content/francesco/en/cotidie/2014/documents/papa-francesco-cotidie_20140320_nameless-man.html.

26. "Pope Francis: Thursday Mass in Santa Marta," Vatican Radio, http://en.radiovaticana.va/news/2015/01/22/pope_francis_thursday_mass_in_santa_marta/1119389.

27. Pope Francis, address, July 26, 2014, https://w2.vatican.va/content/francesco/en/speeches/2014/july/documents/papa-francesco_20140726_clero-caserta.html.

28. Pope Francis, "Pilgrimage to the Holy Land on the Occasion of the 50th Anniversary of the Meeting Between Pope Paul VI and Patriarch Athenagoras in Jerusalem," May 26, 2014.

29. *Dominum et Vivificantem*, 24.

30. *Dominum et Vivificantem*, 41.

31. *Evangelii Gaudium*, 280.

32. Council of Trent. Session XIV—The fourth under the Supreme Pontiff, Julius III, celebrated on the twenty-fifth day of November, 1551.

33. Pope Francis, "God Always Forgives Everything," homily at Santa Marta, *Vatican Radio*, January 23, 2015.

34. Pope Francis, "Address of His Holiness Pope Francis to Participants in a Course on the Internal Forum Organized by the Apostolic Penitentiary," March 12, 2015.

35. Msgr. Peter J. Vaghi, *The Sacraments We Celebrate: A Catholic Guide to the Seven Mysteries of Faith* (South Bend, IN: Ave Maria, 2010), 87.

36. Zenit staff, "General Audience: On the Door of Mercy," Pope Francis, general audience address, Zenit, November 18, 2015.

37. Pope Francis, "Plaza de la Revolución, Holguín," September 21, 2015.

38. Cardinal Walter Kasper, *Mercy: The Essence of the Gospel and the Key to Christian Life* (Mahwah, NJ: Paulist, 2014), 78.

39. Kasper, 82.

40. Pope Francis, "Second Sunday of Easter—Divine Mercy Sunday," April 7, 2013.

41. Pope Francis, "Holy Mass On the Solemnity of Mary, Mother of God," January 1, 2015.

42. Pope Francis, "Holy Mass with the Ordinaries of the Holy Land," May 26, 2014.

43. Cf. Pope Francis, "Holy Mass with the Ordinaries of the Holy Land," 53; Saint Augustine, *De Sancta Virginitate*, III, 3: PL 40, 398; *Sermo* 215, 4; PL 38, 1074; *Sermo* 196, I: PL 38, 1019; *De peccatorum meritis et remissione*, I, 29, 57: PL 44, 142; *Sermo* 25, 7: PL 46, 937–938; Saint Leo the Great, *Tractatus* 21, *de natale Domini*, I: CCL 138, 86.

44. *Redemptoris Mater,* 26.

45. *Redemptoris Mater,* 26.

46. Pope John Paul II, "Mary Prays for the Outpouring of the Spirit," General audience, May 28, 1997.

47. *Redemptoris Mater,* 27.

48. *Redemptoris Mater,* 27.

49. *Redemptoris Mater,* 26.

50. *Redemptoris Mater,* 26.

51. *Verbum Domini*, 15.

52. Pope Francis, "A Traveling Companion." Morning Meditation, Chapel of the Domus Sanctae Marthae, May 6, 2013.

53. *Redemptoris Mater,* 27.

54. *Dominum et Vivificantem*, 25.

55. *Dominum et Vivificantem*, 25.

56. Cardinal Donald Wuerl and Mike Aquilina, *The Feasts: How the Church Year Forms Us as Catholics* (New York: Image, 2014), 89.

57. *Misericordiae Vultus*, 10.

58. *Lumen Fidei*, 31.

59. *Misericordiae Vultus*, 12.

60. *Misericordiae Vultus*, 17.

61. *Evangelii Gaudium*, 15.

62. Pope Francis, "Eucharistic Celebration at the Pontifical North American College," May 2, 2015.

63. *Lumen Fidei,* 31.

Msgr. Peter J. Vaghi is pastor of the Church of the Little Flower in Bethesda, Maryland, and a priest of the Archdiocese of Washington, D.C. He attended seminary at the Pontifical North American College and received his theological education at the Gregorian University, both at Rome. Prior to entry into the seminary, he attended the College of the Holy Cross and later received his law degree at the University of Virginia. He practiced law for a number of years and remains a member of the Virginia State Bar and the District of Columbia Bar.

Msgr. Vaghi is now in his thirtieth year as chaplain of the John Carroll Society, a group of professional and business people in service of the Archbishop of Washington. He is author of the Pillars of Faith series— *The Faith We Profess, The Sacraments We Celebrate, The Commandments We Keep,* and *The Prayer We Offer* in addition to *Encountering Jesus in Word, Sacraments, and Works of Charity*. He has written articles *for America, Columbia, Priest,* and *Our Sunday Visitor*. In addition, he has contributed to two collections of writings on priestly spirituality: *Behold Your Mother* and *Born of the Eucharist*.